INSTANT POT COOKBOOK

The Top Recipes For Everyday Cooking Using Instant
Pot Electric Pressure Cooker

James Diamond

Table of Contents

INTRODUCTION 1

CHAPTER 1 - BREAKFAST 8

Breakfast On-The-Go Eggs Muffin 8

Easy Vanilla Latte Rolled Oats 10

Cheesy Ham and Egg Casserole 11

Instant Pot Apple Crisps Oatmeal 12

Delicious Paleo Bread Pudding 14

Instant Pot Asian Chicken Congee 16

Instant Pot Giant Potato Pancake 18

Instant Pot Scotch Eggs 20

One Pot Chocolate Zucchini Muffins 22

Instant Pot Pumpkin Walnut Bread 24

Instant Pot Hard Boiled Eggs 26

CHAPTER 2 - LUNCH 27

Low Carb Instant Cooker Pork Roast & Brown Mushroom Gravy 27

Instant Pot Ribs with Creamy Coleslaw 29

Spicy Korean Beef over Warm Rice 32

Creamy & Light Butternut Squash Risotto 34

Instant Pot Chuck Roast Dip Sandwiches 36

Instant Pot Spicy Lamb Curry 39

Shredded Salsa Chicken Sandwich 41

Instant Pot Green Bean Casserole 42

Instant Cheesy Chicken Brioche Sandwich 43

Instant Pot Creamy Potato Salad 45

Broccoli and Cheddar Instant Pot Pasta 47

Fast & Creamy Salsa Chicken 48

Basil & Wheat Berry Instant Pot Salad 50

Instant Pot Pineapple Chicken Salad 52

CHAPTER 3 - DINNER 54

Sticky Sweet Honey Teriyaki Chicken 54

Spicy Sticky Paleo Chicken Thighs 56

Instant Cooker Pot Roast 58

Ziti and Cheese with Ground Beef 59

Instant Pot Macaroni and Cheese 60

Salisbury Steak Meatballs 61

Enchilada Pasta 63

Instant Pot Refried Beans with Onion, Garlic and Green Chiles 65

Instant Pulled Pork Carnitas 67

Summer Vegetable Risotto 69

Filipino Instant Pot Chicken Adobo 71

Instant Pot Indian Curried Spinach 73

Instant Pot Smoked Brisket 75

Instant Pot Red Beans and Rice 77

CHAPTER 4 - DESSERTS 79

Decadent Pumpkin Cheesecake 79

Instant Pot Oreo Cheesecake 81

Easy Blueberry Pudding 83

Instant Pot Molten Lava Chocolate Cake 85

Instant Pot Salted Caramel Cheesecake 87

Instant Pot Zesty Key Lime Pie 89

Instant Pot Banana Pumpkin Bundt Cake 91

Instant Pot Pecan Pumpkin Pie 93

Creamy Instant Pot Egg Custard 95

Chocolaty Brownie Instant Pot Cake 97

CHAPTER 5 - VEGAN & VEGETARIAN 99

Kamut, Arugula and Orange Quinoa Salad 99

Instant Pot Refried Beans 101

Healthy Coconut Almond Risotto 103

Fluffy Paleo Banana Bread 104

Indian Red Curry Lentil 106

Vegan One Pot Pasta 108

Instant Pot Potatoes & Chickpeas Curry 110

Instant Pot Vegan Lasagna Soup 112

Polenta in the Instant Pot 114

Vegan Lentil Bolognese in an Instant Pot 115

Instant Pot Mac & Cheese 117

Instant Pot Cranberry Vegan Cake 118

Instant Pot Vegan Posole 120

Vegan Mushroom Risotto 122

CHAPTER 6 - SOUPS, STEWS AND CHOWDERS 124

Instant Pot Stuffed Pepper Soup 124

Instant Pot Gluten Free Minestrone Soup 126

Beef Lentil Instant Pot Stew 128

Creamy Corn Instant Pot Chowder 130

Instant Pot Oxtail Stew 132

Instant Pot Dumplings & Chicken Soup 135

Asian Thai Coconut Chicken Soup 137

Refreshing Summer Squash Soup with Coconut Milk 139

Instant Pot Mexican Albondigas Soup 141

Instant Pot Cod Chowder 143

Instant Pot Creamy Celery Soup 145

Light and Easy Broccoli Soup in the Instant Pot 147

CHAPTER 7- SEAFOOD 149

Instant Pot Seafood Paella 149

Sweet & Spicy Mahi Mahi Instant Pot 151

Wild Alaskan Cod 153

Spicy Lemon Salmon 154

Steamed Asparagus and Shrimp 155

Instant Pot Shrimp Fried Rice 156

Instant Pot Drunken Clams 158

Tiger Prawn Seafood Risotto 160

Instant Pot Jambalaya 162

Instant Pot Orange Ginger Fish 164

CHAPTER 8- SNACKS 165

Dulce de Leche in the Instant Pot 165

Instant Pot Applesauce 167

Creamy Rice Pudding 169

Instant Pot Candied Orange 170

Instant Pot Stuffed Peaches 171

Instant Pot Popcorn 173

Instant Pot Candied Lemon Peel 174

Pressure Cooker Corn on the Cob 175

Pressure Cooker Southern Peanuts 176

Instant Pot Candied Pecans 177

Corn and Jalapeno Dip in an Instant Pot 179

Instant Pot S'mores Brownies 181

CHAPTER 9- RECIPE FOR KIDS 183

Sweet & Sour Chicken 183

Sweet Pork 184

Chicken & Rice Soup.. 185

Spiced Apple Baked Beans 187

Honey Barbeque Chicken Sandwich 188

Grape Jelly BBQ Meatballs... 189

Instant Pot Tater Tot Casserole 190

Slow Cooker Chili.. 191

Buttery Mashed Potatoes... 193

Instant Pot Cheeseburger Sloppy Joes 194

CONCLUSION...195

Introduction

New ways and methods of cooking are constantly being tested and re-invented to make our lives easier and also to make cooking less of a hassle, especially for those of us who are always on the go, have little time in the kitchen and want delicious and healthy meals without constantly standing at the stove. In comes, this new invention called the Instant Pot Cooker.

What is the Instant Pot Cooker?

Not your average cooker, this multi-tasking cooker works as a rice cooker, yogurt appliance, electric cooker, a slow cooker, sauté pan, steamer and browning pan as well as a warming pot. This all-in-one wonder cooker is impressive particularly as it does so many things in one single pot.

Benefits of Using the Instant Pot Cooker

Seems too good to be true? If you are planning on getting one, here are some quick facts about this cooker:

- **Specification and Characteristics:**

  It cooks meals much faster, and it also offers users the option for a delayed start time which can be programmed. The Instant Pot has intelligent cooking competence that enables it to reach the best cooking results. It can alter cooking time and pressure based on the foods that you put into the pot. This can be anything from vegetables to rice, soup, meats and even desserts. It can also adjust the cooking cycle following the amount of food that you place in the cooking, which is done by measuring the pre-heating length of time.

- **Multi-Functional**

  The great thing about this cooker that many users will be able to identify and agree with is that for just one appliance, it has plenty of functionalities. You can set it to cook or steam or sauté and walk away, which means you have time to do other things, which also means you save plenty of time cooking things which take time such as stew, dried beans, whole grains, and lentils.

- **Space Saver**

It's also a space saver! If your apartment is small and you have an even smaller kitchen, the Instant Pot Cooker is a must have. Imagine having seven different appliances for cooking various things when you don't have the space to keep them all.

- **Easy and Safe to use**

Not only does it come in a convenient size, but this wonder pressure cooker also comes with ten built-in safety features and mechanisms that make it easy and extremely safe to use. No need to worry about explosions or rattling noises.

- **Nutritious, Healthy and Tasty Food**

Since the Instant Pot Cooker takes considerably less time to cook, it uses less liquid, thus locking in nutrients to ensure that food is more flavorful. This pressure cooker is also fantastic for softening tough pieces of meat such as beef. Time and again, you will get consistently tasty, tender and delicious meats with this pot.

- **The Quiet Cooker**

Small apartments and homes especially in hotter climates or during the summer can benefit from this. Not only can you set and walk away, you also get to cook without heating up the kitchen and turning it into a hot sauna. It is built to fully seal when pressure builds up leaving no unwanted smell or steam from escaping and indeed no heat.

- **Affordable**

  The prices that the Instant Pot Cooker retails on Amazon are within the range for $120 to $180. Pretty affordable considering that it has that many benefits and can do seven types of cooking methods. It gives you more value, saves time and cooks a range of delicious and healthy meals.

Who Would Want This?

- Anyone who intends to own a pressure cooker, a rice cooker, a slow cooker, a steam and a sauté pot but have nowhere to keep all these items.

- Those who want convenient cooking

- Those who want to 'set it up and forget it' till the timer goes off

- Anyone who prefers one pot meals

- Busy parents and working adults who have packed schedules and many mouths to feed

- Those who want healthy and nutritious meals that can be whipped up quickly, freeing up time for the gym

- People who want to avoid the hassle of having to wash many pots, pans, and equipment to make a simple dinner

- Those who have tiny spaces but desire to cook extravagant dishes

- People who are learning how to cook and do not want to be overwhelmed with too any cooking equipment

How to use the Instant Pot Cooker?

When you look at the cooker, it can be pretty intimidating as there's plenty of buttons and settings. So let's start with the various buttons that most people will usually use:

Keep Warm/Cancel Button

This button is pretty self-explanatory. You press this button to either cancel a cooking function or if you want to switch off your Instant Pot. You can also click on the Adjust button to increase and even reduce the heat of the Pot.

Sauté Button

This function is to sauté your ingredients inside the pot, just as how you sauté things in a pot. You can also click the Adjust button and Sauté button for more charring and to a simmer, you press the Adjust and Sauté button twice.

Manual Button

This button has an all-purpose function. If your recipe mentions cooking on high-pressure for a specific cook time- use this button. You can adjust the cooking time with the '+' or '-indicators. There are also pre-set buttons that you can use instead of the manual one. Most pressure cooking recipes already come with instructions on how many hours and minutes you need to cook a meal for. But with the Instant Cooker Pot, it makes your life easier if in the event you do not have any available recipes or if you want to build or make something from scratch. The preset buttons guide you into determining the amount of time needed for an individual meal.

Here's a list of these buttons and what they can do for pressure cooking:

To make a soup:

For delicious soups, pressure-cook them on high for 30 minutes cook time. All you need to do is put all your ingredients in the pot, press the 'Soup' time and the 'Adjust' button once (more) increase cook time to forty minutes. If you want to cook for twenty minutes, press 'Soup' and 'Adjust' twice (less) to cook for less time. No more slaving over the stove to make the perfect soup.

For meat & stews:

High-pressure cook time is required for 35 minutes for meats and stews, so the meat drops off the bone. To adjust more, click on Adjust more to cook for 45 minutes and to cook less, adjust less to cook for 20 minutes.

For Beans & Chili:

A 30 minute cook time on high-pressure is required. To add more time, press 'Adjust' '+' to increase to 45 minutes and '-' to decrease to 25 minutes. The Instant Pot cuts the time in half when making chili.

For Poultry:

You want the meat tender but not too flaky so the cook time for this is 15 minutes of high pressure. Of course, you can adjust to a 30 minute cook time with '+' or 25 minute cook time with '-.'

For Rice

Rice needs to be fluffy. Too much water and it's lumpy and too little water will make your rice undercooked and dry. The rice function is the only fully automatic programming on the Instant Pot Cooker. The electronic programming adjusts cooking time depending on the ratio of water and rice that you put in the cooking pot.

For Multi-Grain

Ideal to be cooked on high pressure for 40 minutes cook time. If you need to soak them, and then adjust the timer to 45 minutes soaking and 60 minutes cook time.

For Porridge and Congee

The texture you are looking for is soft and somewhat lumpy. Cook on high pressure for 20 minutes. To add more tie, press Adjust '+' to cook for 30 minutes. For less adjust '-for 15 min cook time.

For Steaming

Use a steamer basket or a rack for this function because you want to prevent the food from having to touch the bottom of the pot when it heats at full power. You can cook on high pressure for just 10 minutes. Once the pot reaches the desired pressure, the steam button automatically regulates pressure. Use the '+' or '-buttons to adjust cook time or use the Pressure button to change the fixed timing for lower or higher temperature.

Points to Take note of:

All Instant Pot cookers have pre-sets cooking time set at high-pressure except for the 'Rice' function which uses low pressure.

Apart from the buttons above, you also have on your Instant Pot Cooker:

The Instant Pot switch which is set to default to a four hour slow cooking time. You can adjust the buttons to slow cook at 190 to 210 degree Fahrenheit (88°C - 99°C) for low pressure, 194 to 205 degree Fahrenheit (90°C - 96°C) to normal pressure and 199 to 210 degree Fahrenheit (93°C - 99°C) for high pressure.

Again use, the "+" and "-" buttons to adjust the cooking time accordingly to your desired doneness.

The Pressure button which switches to low or high pressure.

The Yogurt button to make amazing homemade yogurt and can be set to low or high pressure.

The Timer button which is ideal for delayed cooking. Depending on what you are cooking, you need to select a cooking function first, and the make the necessary adjustments. Next, press the timer button and the adjust button to set more or less cook time with then "+" and "-" buttons.

CONCLUSION

The bottom line is, while the Instant Pot Cooker may look intimidating with the variety of buttons, it is actually very easy to use. Once you try your hand at making simple foods to test the buttons, pressure, and settings, you'd be using it so often to make a variety of dishes from breakfast porridges, fluffy omelets, fluffy rice, delicious soups and stews and succulent meat. Not only that, there are plenty of desserts for the perfect ending to a fabulous dinner.

So essentially, this pot can do various types of meals with just one simple equipment.

In the next few chapters, we will explore the variety of recipes that you can make quickly and easily, resulting in a satisfying, delicious and nutritious meal for your friends and family. These recipes are easy to make, fast to cook and above all taste delicious. Perfect for on-the-go families, busy parents with kids and overall anyone looking for simple meals to be done quickly.

Chapter 1 - Breakfast

Breakfast On-The-Go Eggs Muffin

Total Preparation & Cook Time: 40 Minutes

Servings – 6

Nutritional Info: Calories: 308, Fats: 20.5g, Carbs: 5.8g, Protein: 23.8g, Fiber: 0.5g, Sugar: 0.2g

Ingredients:

- 4 free range organic eggs
- ¼ tsp lemon seasoning
- 4 tbsp sharp cheddar, shredded
- 1 green onion, julienned
- 4 slices pre-cooked bacon, sliced

Directions:

1. In the cooker pot, place steamer basket and add 1 ½ cups of water

2. In a large measuring bowl, break eggs, add seasoning and beat till well combined

3. Divide cheese, bacon, and green onion evenly between six muffin cups

4. Pour egg mixture into muffin cup and stir to combine ingredients evenly

5. Place muffin cups on the steamer basket, cover and lock lid in place

6. Select High-pressure cooking for eight minutes cooks

time.

7. When timer goes off, wait a few minutes then use quick pressure to release

8. Lift out steamer basket to remove muffin cups.

9. Serve immediately. Muffins can keep more than a week in the fridge.

Easy Vanilla Latte Rolled Oats

Total Preparation & Cook Time: 20 Minutes

Servings – 4

Nutritional Info: Calories: 100, Fats: 15.1g, Carbs: 7.4g, Protein: 2.4g, Fiber: 5.2g, Sugar: 2.7g

Ingredients:

- 2 ½ cups water
- 1 cup almond or full cream milk
- 1 cup rolled organic oats
- 1 tsp espresso powder
- 2 tsp vanilla extract
- 2 tbsp fine brown sugar
- ¼ tsp salt

Optional: whipped cream and finely grated chocolate

Directions:

1. Combine milk, water, oats, sugar, espresso powder and salt to the pressure cooking pot. Stir the espresso powder to dissolve.
2. Lock the lid and let pot cook on high pressure for 10 minutes.
3. When cooking time is done, switch it off and use naturally release the pressure for about 10 minutes.
4. Release any remaining pressure after the 10 minutes and carefully remove the lid.
5. Stir in vanilla extract and add in additional sugar to taste.
6. Cover pot and let it sit for another five minutes till oats reach desired thickness.
7. To serve, top with whipped cream and grated dark chocolate.

Cheesy Ham and Egg Casserole

Total Preparation & Cook Time: 4 Hours

Servings – 6

Nutritional Info: Calories: 350, Fats: 35.1g, Carbs: 37.4g, Protein: 22.4g, Fiber: 15.7g, Sugar: 10.7g

Ingredients:

- 32 oz cubed hash browns
- 1 large white onion diced
- 2 cups chopped ham
- 10 free-range eggs
- 1 cup whole milk
- 1 ½ cups shredded cheddar cheese

Directions:

1. Prepare the pot of the Instant Cooker with nonstick cooking spray

2. Place ½ hash browns at the bottom and top it with quarter onions, quarter ham, and quarter cheese. Repeat this combination two more times.

3. Combine the pepper, milk, salt and eggs together before mixing thoroughly and adding everything in the cooker.

4. Place pot into Cooker and press 'Slow Cooker' button and the press 'Adjust' to adjust to 3 to 4 hours.

5. Once the cooker starts beeping, release pressure naturally. Serve immediately.

Instant Pot Apple Crisps Oatmeal

Total Preparation & Cook Time: 13 minutes

Servings – 6

Nutritional Info: Calories: 230, Fats: 15.1g, Carbs: 45.4g, Protein: 33.4g, Fiber: 10.7g, Sugar: 8.2g

Ingredients:

- 5 large apples, peeled and chopped into chunks
- ½ cup water
- 1 tbsp maple syrup
- 4 tbsp butter, melted
- ¾ cup rolled oats
- 2 tsp cinnamon
- ¼ cup flour
- ¼ cup brown sugar
- ½ tsp nutmeg
- ½ tsp salt

Directions:

1. Place apple chunks at the bottom of the pot and sprinkle cinnamon and nutmeg.
2. Add in water and maple syrup
3. In a small mixing bowl, stir well oats, melted butter, flour, salt as well as brown sugar
4. Slowly drop by the spoonful the oat combination on top of the apples

5. Secure then seal the instant pot. Manually set the pot to high pressure for 8 minutes cook time.

6. When the pot starts beeping, allow for a natural pressure release and let sit for a few minutes till the sauce thickens.

7. Serve warm

Delicious Paleo Bread Pudding

Total Preparation & Cook Time: 45 minutes

Servings – 10

Nutritional Info: Calories: 300, Fats: 3.5g, Carbs: 20.4, Protein: 60.4g, Fiber: 20.7g, Sugar: 3.5g

Ingredients:

- 1 grain-free loaf bread
- 2 cups high-fat coconut milk
- 4 free range eggs
- 1 tbsp organic vanilla extract
- ½ cup organic maple syrup
- 2 free-range eggs, yolks only
- ¼ tsp pink salt

Directions:

1. Prepare a pot that is slightly smaller than the Instant pot with parchment paper.
2. Cut bread into one-inch cubes and place cubes into lined pot
3. In a blender, place milk, eggs, yolks, syrup, vanilla and salt. Blend for 10 to 15 seconds. Add melted butter and blend thoroughly.
4. In the Instant pot, add water. Add trivet to the pot and place lined the pot with bread on top.
5. Pour blended custard mixture into the pot, pressing gently on the bread to distribute custard evenly.

6. Insert a small even square of parchment paper over the pudding. Fold any corners from the bottom piece that is sticking.

7. Seal and lock vent. Press 'Steam' and 'Adjust' to 15 minutes cook time.

8. When beeper goes off, naturally release pressure for 20 minutes then press 'Cancel' and open pot.

9. Once the pot is slightly cooled, remove inner pot and lift pudding by the corners of the parchment lining the bowl.

10. Transfer pudding to a place and flip over, so the bottom is at the top.

11. Slice and serve with caramelized pears and whipped cream.

Instant Pot Asian Chicken Congee

Total Preparation & Cook Time: 70 minutes

Servings – 4

Nutritional Info: Calories: 210, Fats: 142g, Carbs: 0g, Protein: 8.1g, Fiber: 0g, Sugar: 0g

Ingredients:

- 1 cup jasmine rice, uncooked
- 2 cloves garlic
- 1-inch ginger
- 3 cups shiitake mushrooms
- 2 lb chicken thigh pieces
- 7 cups water
- ½ tbsp salt

Toppings:

- 3 green onions, sliced
- Handful cilantro
- 1 tbsp soy sauce
- 1 tbsp sesame oil, toasted
- ⅓ cup peanuts

Directions:

1. Crush garlic cloves, peel and slice ginger, slice the mushrooms into thin strips

2. Clean and remove skin from the chicken

3. Layer pot by placing rice at the bottom and then the crushed garlic sliced ginger and sliced mushrooms. Place chicken right at the top.

4. Pour in the seven cups of water

5. Lock and seal the lid. Press 'Porridge' to begin cooking. No need to adjust time.

6. Once the cooker reaches the desired temperature and pressure, it will countdown 20 minutes. The pot will beep after 20 minutes and turn to 'keep warm' setting, and the pressure will drop gradually. Allow pressure to release naturally without opening steam valve.

7. Once the float valve falls back to the down position, open the steam valve and then the lid.

8. Remove chicken pieces and place them on cutting board. Use forks to remove the meat off the bones and then shred finely. Place shredded meat back into the pot.

9. Stir porridge to combine all ingredients and add salt as needed, to amplify flavors. Serve congee with a drizzle of healthy dose of sesame oil and soy sauce. Sprinkle green onions, cilantro and chopped peanuts to serve.

Instant Pot Giant Potato Pancake

Total Preparation & Cook Time: 15 minutes

Servings – 6

Nutritional Info: Calories: 927, Fats: 82g, Carbs: 118, Protein: 84g, Fiber: 111.7g, Sugar: 9g

Ingredients:

- 1 egg, beaten
- 1 cup water, cold
- ¾ cup dry potato shreds
- ½ tsp salt
- 1 tbsp chives, chopped
- 1 pinch black pepper, freshly ground
- 1 tsp cayenne pepper,
- 1 tbsp vegetable oil
- 1 tbsp butter
- 1 tbsp chives, chopped
- ¼ cup sour cream for garnish

Directions:

1. In a large bowl, whisk together the salt, water and egg. Make sure that the salt has dissolved.

2. Next, toss in the potatoes and combine. Toss in the chopped chives next followed by a good seasoning of pepper and cayenne. Add more if desired.

3. Preheat your instant pot and click to sauté. Add a little

butter and make sure the pan is well coated with the butter.

4. Pour in your pancake batter into the instant pot and cook on high for 10 to 15 minutes, until the top of the pancake has browned evenly.

5. Use a toothpick to check if the pancake has cooked at the center. If not, add another 5 minutes of cook time.

6. Run a knife along the pan to loosen the edges and tip the pan.

7. The giant pancake should come out easily.

8. Serve with sour cream and garnish with remaining chives.

Instant Pot Scotch Eggs

Total Preparation & Cook Time: 10 minutes

Servings – 4

Nutritional Info: Calories: 1650, Fats: 3.5g, Carbs: 20.4, Protein: 60.4g, Fiber: 20.7g, Sugar: 3.5g

Ingredients:

- 4 large free range eggs
- 1 lb ground meat
- 1 tbsp organic coconut oil

Directions:

1. Place steamer basket inside the pressure cooker. Add one cup water and put eggs in the basket.

2. Close the Pot and lock it. Then cook on high pressure for 6 minutes. Walk away.

3. When the timer goes off, allow for natural pressure release.

4. Turn of Instant pot and allow for quick pressure release. Remove steamer basket from pot and place eggs in an ice bath.

5. Remove shells once eggs have cooled.

6. Divide the sausage into equal pieces of four and flatten them with clean fingers or the back of the spatula into a round shape.

7. Place one egg in each sausage center and wrap gently around the egg.

8. Turn on Instant Pot and click on Sauté. Add oil and

brown the Scotch eggs evenly on all sides.

9. Remove eggs and add one cup of water into Instant Pot. Place insert into the bottom of the pan and arrange eggs carefully on top.

10. Close and lock the lid again and cook for 6 minutes on high pressure.

11. When the timer goes off, do a quick pressure release.

One Pot Chocolate Zucchini Muffins

Total Preparation & Cook Time: 15 minutes

Servings – 6

Nutritional Info: Calories: 1570, Fats: 124.1g, Carbs: 110.5g, Protein: 17.4g, Fiber: 14.0g, Sugar: 3.7g

Ingredients:

- 2 eggs
- ¾ to 1 cup evaporated cane juice
- ½ cup coconut oil
- 3 tbsp unsweetened cocoa powder
- 1 cup flour
- 1 tbsp butter, melted
- ¾ tsp cinnamon
- ¼ tsp sea salt
- 2 tsp vanilla extract
- 1 cup zucchini (or squash), grated
- ⅓ cup chocolate chips
- 1 cup water
- ½ tsp baking soda

Directions:

1. In a clean bowl, use a hand whisk and whisk well eggs, sweetener, vanilla extract and coconut oil. In a separate bowl, mix melted butter together with cocoa powder

until you achieve a smooth dark paste.

2. Combine both the chocolate blend to the egg blend and stir well.

3. To this bowl, sprinkle in the cinnamon, baking soda, salt, and gently fold in the flour.

4. Combine all ingredients well and then toss the grated zucchini and chocolate chips. Do not over stir.

5. Add a trivet to the Instant Pot and pour 1 cup water inside. Fill in your silicone muffin cups with the chocolate zucchini mixture using a small cookie scoop.

6. Layer muffin cups inside the Instant Pot. Once the bottom layer is full, place a parchment paper and piece of aluminum foil on top, cut into a circle to fit the size of the pot.

7. Place another trivet and layer another set of muffin cups. Keep all muffin cups level. Again, cover this layer with aluminum foil and parchment paper

8. Seal and lock the Pot and set on high pressure to cook on for 8 minutes.

9. After cooking is done, allow for natural pressure release, 10minutes.

10. Release valve to remove any remaining pressure.

11. Check for doneness with a toothpick. Remove the cooked muffins from the pot prior to allow them to cool properly

12. Top with cream cheese frosting to serve.

Instant Pot Pumpkin Walnut Bread

Total Preparation & Cook Time: 10 minutes

Servings – 8 servings

Nutritional Info: Calories: 59, Fats: 2.4g, Carbs: 5.3, Protein: 16.5g, Fiber: 22g, Sugar: 3.9g

Ingredients:

- 2 cups pumpkin, pureed
- ½ cup butter at room temperature
- 2 cups flour
- 1.5 tsp baking soda
- 2 eggs at room temperature
- ½ tsp salt
- 1 cup coarse sugar
- 1 cup walnuts

Directions:

1. In a bowl, combine the butter, eggs and sugar

2. Using an electric mixer beat this combination at high speed till you achieve a light and creamy consistency. Scrape the sides of the bowl so that the sugar is incorporated well with the eggs and butter.

3. Add in the pumpkin puree and fold to combine.

4. Toss in your flour and salt and beat again to combine.

5. Next, fold in the walnuts.

6. Using a 6 cup Bundt pan, line and grease it to ensure

smooth removal of the bread.

7. Next, pour in the batter and level it.

8. Before placing the pan in, pour in 1 ½ cups of water into the Instant pot and then place a trivet in it. Your bundt pan should be placed on top of the trivet.

9. Cover the pan with a paper towel and then a piece of foil. This is to prevent water droplets from entering the cake while it is cooking.

10. Close and lock the lid then close the pressure valve too.

11. Bake on high pressure for 55 to 60 minutes. Once the beeper goes off, allow for natural pressure release for at least 10 minutes.

12. Allow the bread to cool in the pan. Once it is cooled, run a knife through the sides to release and serve on a plate.

Instant Pot Hard Boiled Eggs

Total Preparation & Cook Time: 10 minutes

Servings – As many as prepared

Nutritional Info: Calories: 63, Fats: 4.4g, Carbs: 0.3, Protein: 5.5g, Fiber: 0g, Sugar: 0g

Ingredients:

- Eggs, as many as you like
- 1 cup water

Directions:

1. Into the Instant Pot, pour plain water and insert the eggs in a steamer basket.

2. Place steamer basket into the pot and cook, covered approximately 5 minutes using a high pressure.

3. Give the pressure time to release naturally once it is done cooking and then do a quick pressure release.

4. Place hot eggs in an ice bath to stop cooking process.

5. Peel eggs and enjoy!

Chapter 2 - Lunch

Low Carb Instant Cooker Pork Roast & Brown Mushroom Gravy

Total Preparation & Cook Time: 3 hours 10 minutes

Servings – 6

Nutritional Info: Calories: 210, Fats: 1.5g, Carbs: 17g, Protein: 45.4g, Fiber: 23g, Sugar: 2.2g

Ingredients:

- 3 lb fatty cut pork roast
- 2 tbsp coconut oil or ghee
- 1 tsp Celtic salt
- ½ tsp freshly cracked black pepper
- 2 ribs celery
- 4 cups cauliflower, chopped
- 1 large onion, chopped
- 4 garlic cloves, smashed
- 10 Portobello mushrooms, thinly sliced
- 2 cups water

Directions:

1. At the bottom of the pot, arrange the cauliflowers, then spread the onions, garlic, and celery and pour the water in. Top off the Instant Pot layering with the pork roast before using seasoning as desired.

2. Pressurize and let the meal cook for an hour and then depressurize immediately following the beep.

3. Remove pork roast once cooking is done and set aside.

4. Meanwhile, transfer the cooked veggies and broth to your blender and blend until smooth. Set aside.

5. Meanwhile transfer pork roast back into Instant pot and slow cook for 2 hours on high-pressure. This is to crisp the edges of the pork and render the fat.

6. Once the pot roast is done, remove the roast to sit in a safe oven dish. On the 'Sauté' function, cook the mushrooms in coconut oil until soft for 5minutes. Add in the blended vegetables and cook until desired thickness is achieved.

7. Serve roast pork with mushroom gravy.

Instant Pot Ribs with Creamy Coleslaw

Total Preparation & Cook Time: 1 hour 7 minutes

Servings – 4

Nutritional Info: Calories: 780, Fats: 88g, Carbs: 67g, Protein: 52g, Fiber: 100g, Sugar: 6.2g

Ingredients:

- ½ tsp chili powder
- 2 ½ lb baby back ribs
- Salt, to taste
- ¼ tsp paprika
- ⅓ tsp garlic powder

For the BBQ sauce:

- 8 oz tomato paste
- ½ apple juice, natural 2 slices bacon, crumbled
- ½ onion, chopped
- ¼ cup + 1 tbsp coconut oil
- ½ tsp paprika
- Black pepper, to taste
- Salt, to taste
- 1 tbsp ghee
- ¾ cup tomato sauce
- 1 ½ minced garlic cloves

- ⅓ tsp cayenne pepper

- ½ cup cider vinegar

For the coleslaw:

1. ½ half head green organic cabbage, shredded

2. 2 green onions, julienned

3. ½ half red cabbage, shredded

4. 1 cup dry raisins

5. 2/3 cup sweet mayonnaise

6. 2 carrots, shredded

7. ¼ cup organic ACV

8. Celtic salt and pepper

Directions:

To make the coleslaw:

1. Combine the onions, carrots, cabbage, and raisins together in a medium-sized bowl.

2. In another smaller one, mix well the mayonnaise, caraway seeds, and ACV and season as needed.

3. Add the contents of the second bowl to the contents of the first and mix well. Cover and refrigerate till time to serve.

To make the dry rub:

1. To make the dry rub, mix onion powder, paprika, garlic powder, chili powder, pepper, salt and dry mustard.

2. Cut the ribs into smaller slabs to fit into the Instant Cooker. Coat the ribs with the dry rub generously and

place them into the pot.

3. Add the minimum amount of water needed and insert the cooking rack. Place the ribs insides, loosely stacking them.

4. Place the lid and seal it. Cook for 17 minutes, on high pressure.

5. After 15 minutes is done and the ribs have cooked to perfection, allow for release the pressure naturally and then remove the lid.

6. Move ribs to a clean plate, take out the cooking rack and discard any liquid from the pot.

To make the BBQ Sauce:

1. Click 'Sauté' to heat up the pot over low-pressure and add the bacon and cook until its crisp.

2. Toss the garlic and the onion, sautéing for 5 minutes till onions have brown and are soft. Combine all the other items for the sauce and stir well to mix everything. Let simmer for another 10 minutes.

3. Add ribs into the BBQ sauce and make sure to evenly coat so all the ribs are coated fully.

4. Cook for an additional 10 minutes using a high pressure.

5. Release valve to let go of pressure after 10 minutes and transfer ribs to serving dish.

6. Serve ribs warm with a side of coleslaw.

Spicy Korean Beef over Warm Rice

Total Preparation & Cook Time: 1 hour

Servings – 6

Nutritional Info: Calories: 550, Fats: 35.1g, Carbs: 55.4g, Protein: 43.4g, Fiber: 110g, Sugar: 10g

Ingredients:

- 4 lb bottom roast, cubed

- 1 apple, peeled and chopped

- Pepper & salt to season

- 2 tbsp olive oil

- 1 tbsp fresh ginger, grated

- 1 ⅓ cup beef broth

- ½ cup soy sauce, low sodium

- 5 garlic cloves, minced

- 1 tbsp fresh ginger, grated

- 1 large orange, freshly juiced

Directions:

1. Season thawed cubed roast generously with salt and pepper.

2. Heat Instant Pot with 'Sauté' button. Coat hot pan with olive oil.

3. Brown roast in batches, on all sides. Transfer to a plate.

4. De-glaze pan with beef broth, scraping up browned bits.

5. Add in soy sauce and stir.

6. Return browned meat to the pan and spread garlic, ginger, and apples on top of meat.

7. Add in orange juice and lightly stir to combine.

8. Place lid and seal, close the valve. Using 'Manual' button on normal pressure and set to 45 minutes cook time.

9. Once cooking is done and the timer goes off, release steam and shred the meat using a fork. Stir meat together with gravy inside pot to combine.

10. Serve warm over cooked rice.

Creamy & Light Butternut Squash Risotto

Total Preparation & Cook Time: 30 minutes

Servings – 6

Nutritional Info: Calories: 410, Fats: 12g, Carbs: 23.5g, Protein: 11.7g, Fiber: 22.8g, Sugar: 0.7g

Ingredients:

- ½ tsp coriander
- ½ cup white wine
- ¼ tsp oregano
- 3 cloves of minced garlic
- Diced red pepper
- About 3 cups chard, kale and spinach mixture
- Salt, to taste
- Parsley, 1 handful
- 1 ½ tbsp yeast
- 1 tbsp olive oil for sautéing vegetables
- ½ cup chopped yellow onions
- 3 ½ cups vegetable broth, divided
- 2 cups risotto rice
- 1 package white mushrooms
- 1 ½ cups butternut squash
- Pepper, to taste

Directions:

1. Choose the 'Sauté' option on your Instant Pot and add oil

2. When pot it slightly hot, add in bell peppers, onions, garlic, and butternut squash to sauté for 6 minutes till soft and onions have browned.

3. Add in risotto rice and combine

4. Add in vegetable broth, mushrooms, wine, salt, and pepper. Stir to combine.

5. After 6 minutes, add in oregano and coriander. Stir well.

6. Close life and valve. Press 'Manual' and reduce cooking time to 5 minutes.

7. When timer goes off, release pressure immediately and stir in parsley and nutritional yeast as well as greens.

8. Let site for 5 minutes to thicken.

9. Serve warm.

Instant Pot Chuck Roast Dip Sandwiches

Total Preparation & Cook Time: 2 hours 32 minutes

Servings – 7

Nutritional Info: Calories: 620, Fats: 22.3g, Carbs: 54.7g, Protein: 39g, Fiber: 44.8g, Sugar: 10.7g

Ingredients:

- 2 ½ lb chuck roast
- Black pepper to taste
- 1 onion, sliced
- ½ tsp of garlic powder
- ½ cup red wine
- 14 oz beef broth
- 1 dried bay leaf
- 6 soft rolls
- 1 tbsp vegetable oil
- 3 tbsp of unsalted butter, melted
- Pinch of sea salt
- 6 slices of provolone cheese
- ¼ tsp of garlic powder

Directions:

1. Generously flavor chuck roast with pepper and garlic powder and salt on all sides. Let roast sit at room temperature for 15 minutes.

2. After 15minutes, add oil to Instant pot and press 'Sauté.'

3. Flame roast on all sides in the pot using a long heat-proof kitchen tongs.

4. Remove roast and set aside.

5. Toss onions to the pot and sauté till they soften and slightly browned. Add in red wine and let simmer until liquid is reduced to half.

6. Scrap the browned and seared bits from the bottom as the liquid is simmering.

7. Once the wine has reduced, add in low-sodium beef broth and bay leaf.

8. Transfer the roast back into the pot, close lid and seal valve.

9. Hit 'Meat/Stew' button and increase the time to 100 minutes cook time.

10. When pot starts beeping, let pressure release naturally, 25minutes. Turn valve to vent, releasing any excess pressure.

11. Take off lid and transfer roast to serving dish and shred with forks.

12. Strain liquid into pot through a fine mesh strainer and use for dipping sandwiches.

13. Clean out the instant pot and set to 'multigrain.'

14. Combine salt, melted butter, garlic powder in a small bowl.

15. Spread this mixture over bread rolls and toast in the pot for a few minutes until all sides are golden brown.

16. Arrange meat on rolls and top with cheese. Place wire

rack inside pot and place rolls to heat until cheese has melted.

17. Top sandwiches with chopped flat-leaf parsley and serve with dipping sauce.

Instant Pot Spicy Lamb Curry

Total Preparation & Cook Time: 35 minutes

Servings – 6

Nutritional Info: Calories: 520, Fats: 33g, Carbs: 29g, Protein: 38.9g, Fiber: 22.9g, Sugar: 1.1g

Ingredients:

- 2 lb cubed lamb meat, use cuts that are good for stews
- 5 cloves garlic, minced
- 2 inches ginger, freshly grated
- Juice of ½ lime
- 1 medium onion diced
- ¼ tsp sea salt
- ½ cup coconut milk
- Pinch of black pepper
- 1 tbsp ghee
- 1 medium zucchini, diced
- 1 can diced tomatoes
- 1 ½ tbsp garam masala
- ¾ tsp turmeric
- 3 medium carrots, sliced
- Cilantro, chopped

Directions:

1. In a container with a lid, add meat, grated ginger, squeezed lime, minced garlic, and coconut milk before seasoning as needed and mixing well. Leave in fridge for 30 minutes' minimum or up to 8 hours.

2. Add meat together with tomatoes with their juice, ghee, garam masala, carrots and onions into the Instant Pot. Lock the lid and seal the valve. Press 'Manual' and high-pressure cook for 20 minutes.

3. Allow pot to naturally release steam after cooking time is up then flip the valve to release remaining steam. Open the lid.

4. Press Instant Pot to 'Sauté' and add zucchini and allow simmering for 6 minutes.

5. Serve lamb curry over cauliflower rice or naan bread and garnish with chopped cilantro.

Shredded Salsa Chicken Sandwich

Total Preparation & Cook Time: 20 minutes

Servings – 6

Nutritional Info: Calories: 223, Fats: 22g, Carbs: 29.5g, Protein: 10.7g, Fiber: 12.8g, Sugar: 0.2g

Ingredients:

- A lb of chicken tenders
- Garlic powder, 1 pinch
- 1 ½ cup homemade salsa
- ⅓ tsp onion seasoning
- Cumin or paprika, to taste
- Fresh jalapenos, diced and seeded
- Pepper and/or salt as needed

Directions:

1. In the Instant Pot, incorporate chicken and all seasoning into the salsa
2. Close the valve and secure the lid
3. Press 'Poultry' and cook on high pressure, 15 minutes
4. Quick release once timer goes off and remove the lid
5. Shred chicken tenders with for and serve with tortillas, cilantro and avocado slices

Instant Pot Green Bean Casserole

Total Preparation & Cook Time: 20 minutes

Servings – 8

Nutritional Info: Calories: 757, Fats: 69.8g, Carbs: 22g, Protein: 19.7g, Fiber: 4.9g, Sugar: 9.7g

Ingredients:

- 1 cup chicken broth
- 1 cup heavy cream
- 12 sliced mushroom
- 1 small onion
- 2 tbsp butter
- 16 oz green beans
- French's yellow onions for garnish

Directions:

1. Set Instant Pot on Sauté mode
2. When pot is hot, melt better and toss in onions and mushrooms, let them cook approximately 3 minutes.
3. Pour in broth, heavy cream, and green beans.
4. Set pot to Manual and for 15 minutes, cook on high pressure then carry out quick release.
5. Add in 2 tbsp of cornstarch to thicken the mixture.
6. To serve, garnish with French onions

Instant Cheesy Chicken Brioche Sandwich

Total Preparation & Cook Time: 40 minutes

Servings – 4

Nutritional Info: Calories: 3307, Fats: 183g, Carbs: 34g, Protein: 307g, Fiber: 0g, Sugar: 0g

Ingredients:

- 3 tbsp corn starch
- 1 packet ranch seasoning
- 1 cup water
- 8 slices cooked crispy bacon
- 2 lb boneless chicken breast
- 4-oz cheddar cheese
- 8-oz cream cheese

Directions:

1. Arrange chicken at the bottom of the Instant Pot and then spread the cream cheese evenly.

2. Sprinkle on the ranch seasoning, making sure to cover the surface area

3. To this, add one cup water.

4. Click on Manual and cook for 25 minutes on high pressure.

5. Once the timer beeps, do a quick pressure release.

6. Remove only the chicken and shred it.

7. Make sure Instant Pot in on low. Mix in cornstarch with

43

a whisk to avoid any clumps.

8. Add in cheese and then the shredded chicken.

9. Stir in bacon and stir once more for all ingredients to be well incorporated.

10. Serve cheese chicken on toasted brioche buns

Instant Pot Creamy Potato Salad

Total Preparation & Cook Time: 10 minutes

Servings – 8

Nutritional Info: Calories: 1968, Fats: 100g, Carbs: 29.5g, Protein: 45g, Fiber: 20g, Sugar: 30g

Ingredients:

- 6 medium potatoes, peeled and cubed
- Salt, as needed
- 1 tbsp fresh dill
- 1 cup mayonnaise
- 4 free-range eggs
- ¼ cup onion, chopped
- Pepper, as needed
- 2 tbsp dill pickle juice
- 1 tbsp ground mustard
- 1 tbsp parsley
- ¾ cups water

Directions:

1. Add water to the Instant pot then place a steamer basket inside

2. Pour water into the pot and place potatoes and eggs to the steamer basket.

3. Lock the lid and click on Manual. Cook on High Pressure for 4 minutes.

4. Once beeper goes off, perform quick release.

5. Turn off Instant Pot and remove the lid.

6. Place eggs in an ice bath to stop cooking process then place potatoes into a serving dish.

7. Combine dressing ingredients.

8. Once eggs are cooled, peel and dice to mix into salad.

9. Check for taste and season with salt and pepper.

10. Chop and sprinkle parsley to the top.

11. Refrigerate salad before serving.

Broccoli and Cheddar Instant Pot Pasta

Total Preparation & Cook Time: 20 minutes

Servings – 6

Nutritional Info: Calories: 3223, Fats: 172g, Carbs: 226.5g, Protein: 197g, Fiber: 0g, Sugar: 0g

Ingredients:

- 1 lb of pasta
- 4 cups water
- 16 oz cheddar cheese
- 16 oz bag frozen broccoli
- 1 cup full cream milk
- 1 lb grilled chicken breast

Directions:

1. In your Instant Pot, pour in 4 cups of water and then your pasta.
2. Top this with frozen broccoli.
3. Place the pot on Manual and cook on high pressure for 4 minutes.
4. Perform quick release and the switch mode to Sauté.
5. Pour in milk and cheese and stir pasta till cheese has melted.
6. Stir in grilled chicken breast
7. Serve hot.

Fast & Creamy Salsa Chicken

Total Preparation & Cook Time: 20 minutes

Servings – 6

Nutritional info: Calories: 3172, Fats: 134.7g, Carbs: 23.9g, Protein: 424g, Fiber: 4.8g, Sugar: 8.9g

Ingredients:

- 3 tsp taco seasoning
- 3 lb chicken breasts
- ½ cup chicken broth
- 1 cup salsa
- 4 oz cream cheese
- ⅓ cups cottage cheese
- Garnish: cheese, sour cream, chopped cilantro, sliced avocado, chopped tomatoes, black beans

Directions:

1. Place chicken and chicken broth into Instant Pot
2. Click on 'poultry' and seal the vent. Cook for 10 minutes.
3. Once done, quick release the lid and check chicken with meat thermometer. The temperature should read 160 degrees.
4. When it is, remove from pot and place in large bowl.
5. Save ½ cup of the broth and discard the rest.
6. Add the brother and the remaining ingredients into the

Instant Pot.

7. Turn to Sauté and add cream cheese and cottage cheese into the pot and beat until cheese has liquefied.

8. Switch to Keep Warm. Shred the cooled chicken and add that back into the sauce. Stir to combine.

9. Serve with shredded cheese, sour cream, avocado, tomatoes, cilantro and black beans.

Basil & Wheat Berry Instant Pot Salad

Total Preparation & Cook Time: 40 minutes

Servings – 6

Nutritional info: Calories: 753, Fats: 43.7g, Carbs: 82.5g, Protein: 18.7g, Fiber: 6.8g, Sugar: 6.3g

Ingredients:

For the wheat berries:

- 1.5 cups wheat berries

- 1 tbsp olive oil

- 4 cups water

- 1 pinch salt

For the salad:

- 1 tbsp balsamic vinegar

- 1-2 oz. feta cheese

- 1 tbsp olive oil

- 2 stalks spring onions, chopped

- ¾ cups chopped grape tomatoes

- 1 cup fresh basil and fresh parsley, chopped

- ⅓ cup chopped olives

Directions:

1. Add olive oil to Instant Pot and click on Sauté. Toast wheat berries so it has a nutty flavor

2. When the berries are fragrant, add water and salt.

3. Press Cancel to stop Sauté mode and click on Manual. Cook for 36 minutes using a high pressure.

4. When cooking is done, allow for natural pressure release for 10 minutes. Then open the valve and the lid.

5. Drain the wheat berries and run it under cold water to stop cooking.

6. Place berries into a mixing bowl and toss with left over salad items.

7. Sprinkle with salt and pepper to flavor.

Instant Pot Pineapple Chicken Salad

Total Preparation & Cook Time: 30 minutes

Servings – 6

Nutritional info: Calories: 753, Fats: 43.7g, Carbs: 82.5g, Protein: 18.7g, Fiber: 6.8g, Sugar: 6.3g

Ingredients:

- 2 lb organic chicken thighs sliced into bite-size pieces
- 1 cup fresh pineapple chunks
- ½ cup organic coconut cream
- 1 tsp cinnamon
- ⅛ tsp salt
- 2 tbsp coconut amino
- ½ cup green onions, julienned

Directions:

1. Turn on our Instant Pot
2. Toss all ingredients except green onions into the pot
3. Close and lock the lid
4. Press the Poultry button. Let pot cook and walk away
5. Pot will cook for 15 minutes on high pressure
6. Once the cooking is done, the timer will beep. Turn pot off.
7. Allow pressure to release naturally.
8. Open the lid and stir contents to combine

9. If the sauce is too liquid, thicken it with a tsp of arrowroot starch.

10. Next, click on the Sauté button and then cook the sauce again until it thickens up to your desire.

11. Turn the pot off.

12. Place salad on serving dish and garnish with green onions.

Chapter 3 - Dinner

Sticky Sweet Honey Teriyaki Chicken

Total Preparation & Cook Time: 30 minutes

Servings – 8

Nutritional info: Calories: 203, Fats: 42g, Carbs: 33.5g, Protein: 15.7g, Fiber: 32.8g, Sugar: 5.2g

Ingredients:

- ⅓ cup rice vinegar
- 4 skinless and boneless chicken breast
- ½ cup low-sodium soy sauce
- ½ onion, sliced
- 2/3 tsp ground ginger
- 2 garlic cloves, crushed
- ¼ tsp pepper
- ½ cup organic honey
- 3 tbsp cornstarch
- Sesame seeds, to taste
- ⅓ cups water
- ⅓ cup onion, sliced

Directions:

1. Use non-stick cooking spray to spray the inside of the Instant Pot inner pot

2. Place chicken breasts into the inner pot

3. Whisk together honey, soy sauce, rice vinegar, crushed garlic, onion, and seasonings together and use the results to coat the chicken.

4. Cook for 17 minutes on high pressure. Check to see if chicken is cooked. Once cooled slightly, remove from Instant pot and shred chicken.

5. Combine the water and cornstarch. Slowly incorporate the sauce inside the Instant Pot and press 'Sauté' while whisking the mixture. Allow the pan to sauté for a minutes till the sauce begins to boil and thicken.

6. Turn off pot and place shredded chicken into the pot and stir with the sauce to coat.

7. Serve chicken over rice and garnish with sesame seeds and green onions.

Spicy Sticky Paleo Chicken Thighs

Total Preparation & Cook Time: 30 minutes

Servings – 6

Nutritional info: Calories: 540, Fats: 52g, Carbs: 53.5g, Protein: 85.7g, Fiber: 32.8g, Sugar: 8.2g

Ingredients:

- 3 lb bone-in chicken thighs
- 1 tbsp chipotle powder
- 1 tsp sesame seeds
- 1 tbsp cumin
- ½ tsp cayenne pepper
- 1 tsp coriander
- 1 tsp ginger & 1 tsp garlic powder
- 1 tsp turmeric
- 1 ¾ tbsp lemon juice
- 1 tsp pepper
- 1 tbsp pink salt
- 2 tbsp organic coconut oil
- Cilantro & green onion for garnish
- ¼ cup organic honey
- 2 tbsp blackstrap molasses
- 2 tbsp hot sauce
- 2/3 cup water

Directions:

1. Clean the chicken and tap it dry with a kitchen towel.

2. To make spice rub, combine turmeric, cumin, ginger, coriander, chipotle, garlic, cayenne, salt and pepper. Coat chicken on all sides.

3. Add coconut oil to the pot and click on 'Sauté' without covering the cooker. Brown chicken thighs evenly.

4. Take out chicken from pot and add a little bit of water. Pot will hiss and boil so don't stand too close and wear oven mitts. Once hissing slows down, scrape the brown bits with a kitchen spoon.

5. Add the chicken thighs in again and set the Pot to 'Manual' and adjust timing to 13 minutes. Ensure steam valve is set to 'sealing'. Let cook.

6. While that is happening, combine the Sriracha, honey, molasses and lemon together in a separate bowl.

7. When timer goes off, quick release to vent to stop chicken from cooking. Use wooden spoon to move the valve to prevent burning your hands.

8. Take out lid and use kitchen tongs to remove chicken. Place in dish and cover with foil to keep warm. Turn pot to 'Sauté' with juices still in pot. Pour the honey mixture into the pot and allow mixture to boil, whisking occasionally until sauce has reached desired consistency.

9. When sauce has thickened, turn pot to 'Keep Warm'. Take chicken thighs and dip into sauce to coat on all sides.

10. To serve, garnish with sesame seeds, green onions and cilantro.

Instant Cooker Pot Roast

Total Preparation & Cook Time: 1 hour 46 minutes

Servings – 6

Nutritional info: Calories: 139, Fats: 25g, Carbs: 44g, Protein: 35.7g, Fiber: 22.8g, Sugar: 3.2g

Ingredients:

- 6 lb arm roast
- ½ cup low-sodium beef broth
- ¼ stick butter
- 8 pepperoncini
- ½ pepperoncini juice
- 1 packet ranch dressing mix
- 1 packet gravy mix

Directions:

1. Pour pepperoncini juice and broth into cooker
2. Add roast
3. Sprinkle dressing and gravy mix over roast
4. Top with butter and pepperoncini
5. Cook at high pressure for 90 minutes on 'Manual.'
6. Do not allow warming cycle to kick in
7. Use natural release for 15 minutes and the switch to quick release.
8. Serve with seasonal vegetables and mash

Ziti and Cheese with Ground Beef

Total Preparation & Cook Time: 20 minutes

Servings – 6

Nutritional info: Calories: 1945, Fats: 28g, Carbs: 344g,
Protein: 88.7g, Fiber: 17.8g, Sugar: 18.2g

Ingredients:

- 1 ¼ lb ground beef
- 16 oz ziti
- Pepper, to taste
- Salt, to taste
- 4 oz shredded mozzarella
- 1 small yellow onion
- 1 jar pasta sauce

Directions:

1. Set the Instant Pot to 'Sauté' and use it to cook the onions for three minutes.
2. Brown the beef in the same fashion.
3. Add 1 jar of sauce together with 24 oz. water.
4. Wait 4 minutes before adding in the ziti and switch the pot to 'Steam' for 5minutes.
5. Once the timer goes off, add in the 4 oz of mozzarella.
6. Add in salt and pepper to savor.
7. Take out from pot and serve warm.

Instant Pot Macaroni and Cheese

Total Preparation & Cook Time: 15 minutes

Servings – 6

Nutritional info: Calories: 4237, Fats: 398g, Carbs: 24g, Protein: 152.7g, Fiber: 0g, Sugar: 1.2g

Ingredients:

- ¾ cup half and half
- 1 lb gluten free pasta
- 2 sticks of butter
- ¾ tbsp dry mustard powder
- 3 ¾ cups of water
- 1 cup cheese, Monterey Jack or own choice
- 1 tsp hot sauce

Directions:

1. Place pasta, water, dry mustard and hot sauce into the Instant Pot
2. Pressure cook on high for 4 minutes cook time
3. Perform an instant release to prevent the pasta from cooking further
4. Next, stir in butter, cheeses and half & half and stir slowly to allow the cheese to melt.
5. Serve immediately

Salisbury Steak Meatballs

Total Preparation & Cook Time: 40 minutes

Servings – 4

Nutritional info: Calories: 997, Fats: 42g, Carbs: 25.2g, Protein: 128g, Fiber: 4.3g, Sugar: 11.2g

Ingredients:

- ¼ tsp powdered mustard
- ⅓ cup onions, minced
- ½ cup whole wheat seasoned breadcrumbs
- 5 lb sliced mushrooms, chopped
- 1 large free-range egg, beaten
- ½ lb organic lean ground turkey
- 2 tbsp tomato paste, divided
- 3 tbsp olive oil
- 2 tsp Worcestershire sauce, to taste
- Pinch freshly cracked black pepper
- 1 tbsp wheat flour
- ½ lb beef, ground
- 1 cup beef bouillabaisse
- Roughly chopped parsley, for garnish
- Kosher salt, to taste
- 2 ½ tsp wine vinegar

Directions:

1. Turn Instant Pot on and click on 'Sauté'. Add one tsp of oil and sauté onions till it turns golden brown. Remove from pan and divide onions into two.

2. Mix half of the onions with the ground turkey and beef, chopped mushrooms, bread crumbs, eggs, 1 tbsp of tomato paste and beef broth in a large mixing bowl before seasoning as desired. Shape meat into 20 meatballs and refrigerate to firm.

3. In another bowl, combine flour and one cup of bouillabaisse until smooth. Add in remaining onions and 1 tbsp tomato paste, vinegar, Worcestershire sauce and mustard.

4. Heat the Instant Pot back to sauté and add in remaining tsp of oil cook the meatballs 4 minutes per side.

5. Add all of the ingredients to the cooker and let it cook, covered, at a high pressure 10 minutes.

6. Allow the pressure to release naturally.

7. Serve garnished with parsley and with mashed potatoes.

Enchilada Pasta

Total Preparation & Cook Time: 35 minutes

Servings – 6

Nutritional info: Calories: 1980, Fats: 68.6g, Carbs: 225g, Protein: 28g, Fiber: 90.3g, Sugar: 2.4g

Ingredients:

- 8 oz gluten-free penne pasta
- 12 oz enchilada sauce
- ½ lb ground turkey
- 2 cups chicken or veggie broth
- 1 cup shredded cheese of choice
- 2 tbsp taco seasoning
- ⅓ cup sour cream

Directions:

1. Set the Instant Pot to Sauté and brown the meat with the seasoning

2. Combine the enchilada sauce, pasta and broth into the pot. The liquid ought to barely cover the pasta. Add a little more if it doesn't.

3. Place the lid on and close the valve. Set the pressure on high and cook for 4 minutes.

4. After the timer goes off, let pressure to release on its own for 4 minutes then do a fast release.

5. Stir in cheese and pepper and salt to season.

6. For serving, transfer enchilada pasta to serving dish and top with fresh Mexican queso and black olives.

7. Stir in sour cream for added creaminess.

Instant Pot Refried Beans with Onion, Garlic and Green Chiles

Total Preparation & Cook Time: 40 minutes

Servings – 4

Nutritional info: Calories: 541, Fats: 37.5g, Carbs: 15.2g, Protein: 29.9g, Fiber: 2.6g, Sugar: 5.6g

Ingredients:

- 2 cups soaked pinto beans
- 3 tbsp organic olive oil
- 1 cup yellow onions, chopped
- 1 tbsp garlic, minced
- 1 can diced green chilies
- 1 tsp salt

Directions:

1. In instant pot, add in beans at the bottom and cover with enough water, about 2 inches.
2. Add 1 tbsp olive oil and then lock lid and cook on high pressure for 20 minutes.
3. When timer goes off, let the pressure release on its own
4. Add chopped onions, minced garlic, canned chilies and salt
5. Lock lid again and pressure cook on high for 10 minutes.
6. Release pressure naturally. Remove lid and mash beans to desired consistency. Do not liquefy. Remove beans

from pot.

7. Clean pot and turn to sauté, add beans again and simmer on low heat, stirring often until beans have thickened to desired consistency. About 10 minutes.

Instant Pulled Pork Carnitas

Total Preparation & Cook Time: 1 hour 20 minutes

Servings – 10

Nutritional info: Calories: 160, Fats: 7g, Carbs: 1g, Protein: 20g, Fiber: 0g, Sugar: 11.2g

Ingredients:

- 2 chipotle peppers with adobo sauce
- 2 ½ lb roast
- 2 tsp cumin
- ¾ cup low sodium broth
- ¼ tsp dry adobo seasoning
- ½ tsp garlic powder
- ¼ tsp dry oregano
- 6 slivered cloves of garlic
- 2 leaves of bay
- 2 tsp kosher salt

Directions:

1. Set Instant Pot to Sauté.

2. Season pork generously with salt and pepper. Once pot is nice and hot, sauté all sides of the pork on high-heat for 5 minutes. Remove from pot and allow cooling.

3. With a sharp knife, insert knife blade into pork about 1 inch deep and insert garlic slivers. Make sure both sides of pork have garlic generously spread out evenly.

4. Season pork with oregano, adobo, cumin and garlic powder. Use hands to rub mixture into pork meat.

5. Pour chicken broth into the Instant pot and add in chipotle peppers, bay leaves and stir.

6. Place pork inside and cover lid to cook on high pressure for 50 minutes.

7. When the timer goes off, release pressure and shred pork using forks. Place pork back into pot. Allow pork meat to soak up juices.

8. Remove bay leaves and adjust seasoning. Mix well.

9. Serve with soft taco shells and fresh sliced avocados and some sour cream.

Summer Vegetable Risotto

Total Preparation & Cook Time: 1 hour 20 minutes

Servings – 10

Nutritional info: Calories: 160, Fats: 7g, Carbs: 1g, Protein: 20g, Fiber: 0g, Sugar: 22.3g

Ingredients:

- ¼ a cup of wine, white
- 2 ½ cloves of garlic
- 1 tsp of olive oil
- 1 cup of diced organic zucchini
- Pepper, as needed
- 2 tbsp nutritional yeast
- ⅓ a cup fresh parsley, cut into small pieces
- 1 cup diced organic eggplant
- 2/3 cups onion, minced
- 1 cup diced organic acorn squash
- 2 cups risotto rice
- 1 medium sized tomato diced
- 1 tbsp earth balance butter
- Salt, 1 pinch
- 3 ¾ cups broth separated

Directions:

1. Turn the Instant Pot on and set it to 'sauté before adding in a bit of oil.

2. Add in the garlic along with the onions and then let both cook for approximately 3 minutes.

3. Add in the combination of vegetables- zucchini, eggplant and squash and stir well for about a quarter of an hour until they are nice and soft.

4. Mix in rice and ensure it is well coated in the vegetable mixture.

5. Combine the vegetable broth, salt, pepper, wine, oregano and stir well

6. Close the lid and seal the pressure valve

7. Press 'Manual' and adjust the time to reduce to 5 minutes

8. When the timer starts beeping, release the pressure immediately to prevent over-cooking

9. Stir in nutritional yeast, earth balance, tomatoes and parsley and let sit for another 5 minutes for sauce to thicken.

10. Serve risotto warm and sprinkle fresh parsley as garnish.

Filipino Instant Pot Chicken Adobo

Total Preparation & Cook Time: 40 minutes

Servings – 6

Nutritional info: Calories: 721, Fats: 23.9g, Carbs: 31.5g, Protein: 20g, Fiber: 2.2g, Sugar: 15.9g

Ingredients:

- 6 chicken drumsticks, skin on
- 1 tbsp olive oil
- Green onions julienned for garnish

Sauce:

- ¼ cup Filipino soy sauce
- ½ cup light soy sauce
- ¼ cup Filipino vinegar
- 1 tbsp fish sauce
- 1 tbsp sugar
- 10 garlic cloves, crushed
- 1 small onion, minced
- 1 tsp ground black peppercorn
- 1 dried red chili
- 4 dried bay leaves

Cornstarch mixture (Optional):

- 1 tsp cornstarch
- 1 tbsp water

Directions:

1. Mix together both soy sauce, Filipino vinegar, sugar and fish sauce

2. In the instant Pot, click on Sauté and add the oil to the pot. Once it heats up brown the chicken and remove it.

3. Continue with sautéing the onions and the garlic until fragrant and lightly browned then toss in peppercorns, chili and bay leaves. Sauté for half a minute.

4. Close and lock lid then cook on high pressure for 10 minutes.

5. Once done, naturally release pressure.

6. Place chicken on bed of steamed rice.

Instant Pot Indian Curried Spinach

Total Preparation & Cook Time: 20 minutes

Servings – 6

Nutritional info: Calories: 453, Fats: 28g, Carbs: 44g, Protein: 20g, Fiber: 16.0g, Sugar: 11.3g

Ingredients:

- 1 lb spinach, rinsed
- 1 lb mustard leaves, rinsed
- 2 tbsp ghee
- 2 medium onions, diced
- 2-inch knob ginger, minced
- 4 garlic cloves, minced
- 1 tsp garam masala
- ½ tsp turmeric
- ½ tsp black pepper
- Pinch of dried fenugreek leaves
- ½ tsp cayenne
- 1 tsp coriander
- 1 tsp cumin

Directions:

1. Click on the Sauté button and then melt the ghee
2. Next, add the onions, garlic, ginger and spices and sauté for three minutes.

3. Add in the spinach and continue to sauté till it wilts. Next add the mustard leaves.

4. Click on 'Keep Warm/Cancel' and put the lid one.

5. Press 'Poultry' and let the ingredients cook for 15 minutes.

6. Once the Pot beeps, allow the pressure to release naturally. Cool mixture for a few minute then transfer to blender.

7. Blend to desired consistency and pour the mixture back into the Instant Pot.

8. To serve, place one spoonful of ghee on top and together with warm naan bread.

Instant Pot Smoked Brisket

Total Preparation & Cook Time: 1 hour 15 minutes

Servings – 8

Nutritional info: Calories: 1360, Fats: 43g, Carbs: 21.4g, Protein: 207g, Fiber: 0g, Sugar: 16.5g

Ingredients:

- 1 ½ lb beef brisket
- 2 tbsp maple sugar
- 2 tsp smoked sea salt
- ½ tsp smoked paprika
- 1 tsp mustard powder
- 1 tsp black pepper
- 1 tsp onion powder
- 2 cups low sodium beef broth
- 3 fresh thyme sprigs

Directions

1. Thaw brisket for 30 minutes before cooking. Pat it dry and set aside.

2. Next, make spice blend by mixing maple sugar, sea salt, pepper, onion powder, mustard powder and smoked paprika.

3. Dry rub the meat generously on all sides.

4. Turn on the Instant pot and set it to Sauté. Add some high heat cooking oil and place the brisket inside.

5. Make sure to brown all sides of the brisket till it turns a deep golden color but not till burnt.

6. Place the fatty sides up add pour in the broth and add the thyme into it.

7. Scrape the browned bits and then cover the pot.

8. Click on Manual and increase the cooking time to 50 minutes.

9. When timer goes off, allow for natural release so moisture can help keep the meat supple.

10. Remove brisket from the pot and cover with foil. Leave to rest.

11. Switch pot to Sauté then reduce or thicken the broth inside the pot to make a sauce, about 10 minutes.

12. Once the brisket has cooled down slightly, slice it and serve with steamed vegetables and mash potatoes. Drizzle meat with sauce.

Instant Pot Red Beans and Rice

Total Preparation & Cook Time: 45 minutes

Servings – 10

Nutritional info: Calories: 8463, Fats: 17.3g, Carbs: 177g, Protein: 261g, Fiber: 96.5g, Sugar: 16.3g

Ingredients:

- 10 cups cooked rice
- Salt, to taste
- 2 stalks worth of celery diced
- 3 cloves minced garlic
- Pepper, to taste
- 1 tsp hot sauce
- 2 ½ leaves of bay
- 7 cups water
- 1 onion chopped
- 1 lb dry red kidney beans
- Salt, to taste
- 1 tsp fresh thyme or ½ tsp dried thyme
- 1 lb chicken andouille sausage cut into thin slices
- 1 bell pepper chopped

Directions:

1. Toss all ingredients, except rice and sausage into the Instant Pot.

2. Prepare the instant pot for cooking and cook on high for half an hour.

3. Once done, quick release and turn off valve.

4. Once all pressure is gone, remove the lid off the pot and run it under cold water. Set lid aside.

5. Add sausage into the pot, close and lock lid again.

6. Click on manual and cook on high pressure for 15 minutes. Again, allow pressure to release naturally after cooking.

7. Let beans site in pot with the lid off so the liquid can thicken.

8. Serve beans on steamed white rice.

Chapter 4 - Desserts

Decadent Pumpkin Cheesecake

Total Preparation & Cook Time: 45 minutes

Servings – 6

Nutritional info: Calories: 422, Fats: 0.9g, Carbs: 111g, Protein: 1.5g, Fiber: 0g, Sugar: 104.4g

Ingredients:

For Cheesecake:

- 2 free-range eggs, room temperature

- ½ cup sugar

- 1 box cream cheese

- ½ cup fresh pumpkin

- 1 tsp pumpkin pie spice

- 2/3 box of graham crackers, crushed

- ¼ cups butter – melted

For Topping:

1 milk chocolate bar shaved into curls

Directions:

1. Combine melted butter with crushed graham crackers

2. Spread mixture on bottom of 7" springform pan, using spoon to form an even layer of crust

3. Keep in the freezer to chill while working on the batter.

4. For the batter, combine eggs, pumpkin, cream cheese and sugar into a mixer and mix till well blended, on high until no lumps and mixture are fluffy.

5. Add spices and mix lightly one more time until spices blend well.

6. Pour mixture into the pan with crust.

7. To bake, place 1 cup of water into the Instant Pot and insert trivet. The water level should be enough to create steam but must not touch trivet.

8. Create a sling for cheesecake, take 18" foil piece and fold long way. Place in Instant Pot.

9. Carefully place cheesecake into Instant Pot on the sling, making sure that sling does not touch cheesecake.

10. Put on the lid and select Manual and cook for 25 minutes.

11. Once the timer goes off, quick release steam and remove cheesecake using a sling.

12. Let cool 15 minutes prior to moving to fridge for 8 hours or overnight.

13. To serve, remove cheesecake from the pan and sprinkle with chocolate shavings.

Instant Pot Oreo Cheesecake

Total Preparation & Cook Time: 45 minutes

Servings – 6

Nutritional info: Calories: 1800, Fats: 225g, Carbs: 124g, Protein: 51.1g, Fiber: 0g, Sugar: 102.6g

Ingredients:

For Cheesecake:

- 12 whole Oreo cookies, crushed into crumbs
- 2 tbsp salted butter, melted
- ½ cup sugar
- 2 large eggs
- 2 boxes cream cheese
- 1 tbsp flour
- 2 tsp pure vanilla extract
- 8 whole Oreo cookies, crumbled
- ⅓ cup mixing cream

For the Topping:

- 1 cup whipped cream or whipped topping
- 8 whole Oreo cookies, chopped coarsely
- chocolate sauce, optional

Directions:

1. Prepare 7 inch springform pan by wrapping bottom of pan in foil and greasing as needed.

2. Combine 12 crushed Oreo cookies with the melted butter. Press to form crust at the bottom of springform pan. Place pan in freezer to set.

3. To make the cheesecake, blend the cream cheese until silky. Pour in the sugar and mix till well combined.

4. With the mixer in moderate speed, add in one eggs, incorporating each egg fully before adding the next.

5. Combine flour into mixture, followed by heavy cream and vanilla. Blend till smooth consistency.

6. Add inn 8 chopped Oreos and pour batter into foiled and greased pan. Cover pan with foil.

7. In the Instant pot, add in 1 cup water and place trivet at the bottom.

8. Create foil sling and place pan on top of the sling.

9. Lock lid and seal vent. Press 'Manual' and cook for 40 minutes on high pressure.

10. When timber beeps, allow pressure to release naturally and do a quick release.

11. Remove cheesecake from pot using foil cling, uncover cheesecake and let cool on wire rack at room temperature.

12. Once cake has cooled, refrigerate for 8 hours or all night.

13. To serve, top with whip cream and crumbled Oreo cookies and chocolate drizzle sauce.

Easy Blueberry Pudding

Total Preparation & Cook Time: 30 minutes

Servings – 4

Nutritional info: Calories: 1282, Fats: 102.7g, Carbs: 220g, Protein: 34.1g, Fiber: 11.5g, Sugar: 30.7g

Ingredients:

- ½ lb fresh blueberries
- ¾ tsp baking powder
- ½ cup flour
- ½ cup butter
- 2 tbsp dried breadcrumbs
- Salt, 1 pinch
- ½ granulated sugar
- 1 egg, beaten
- 5 oz milk
- Cream to serve, or cream fraiche
- ¾ cups of flour

Directions:

1. Grease and line a 6 cup pudding basin. Combine baking powder, salt and floor and sift. Mix in butter then add breadcrumbs and sugar. Combine well before stirring in egg and milk.

2. Gently add and stir in blueberries. Pour mixture into basin and fill only three quarters to allow room for

dough to rise

3. Prepare double square parchment paper, large enough so it hangs over the rim of the basin by an inch. Fold pleats into it to allow for expansion. Butter the underside and secure paper with string under the rim. Make a handle for the basin by looking the string over and tying on the opposite side.

4. Heat up 2 inches of water inside the Instant cooker with a steamer inside the bottom.

5. Place basin on steamer and cover cooker without clamping the lid and steam for 15 minutes.

6. After 15 minutes, clamp the lid shut, reduce the heat to the midpoint and cook for another half an hour.

7. When cooking is complete, turn the heat off and vent immediately. Remove basin and run knife along sides to release pudding. Transfer to serving dish.

8. Serve pudding with fresh cream.

Instant Pot Molten Lava Chocolate Cake

Total Preparation & Cook Time: 15 minutes

Servings – 6

Nutritional info: Calories: 631, Fats: 33g, Carbs: 52.5g, Protein: 10.8g, Fiber: 1.0g, Sugar: 51.2g

Ingredients:

- ½ tsp salt
- 1 large egg
- 2 tbsp extra virgin olive oil
- 4 tbsp sugar
- 4 tbsp whole milk
- 4 tbsp all-purpose flour
- 1 tbsp unsweetened cacao
- 2/3 tsp baking powder
- ½ tsp orange zest
- Powdered sugar for decoration

Directions:

1. Using ramekins, prepare them by buttering or oiling the insides.

2. Pour 1 cup of water into the Instant pot and place a trivet inside.

3. Mix all of the ingredients together in a bowl big enough to ensure you combine thoroughly.

4. Add the mixture into prepared ramekins and leave a

little room at the top.

5. Place ramekins inside Pot, close lid and shut the valve.

6. Set pot to cook for 6 minutes for a gooey inside, or 9 minutes for a firmer inside.

7. Once the timer goes off, remove ramekins and leave to cool

8. To serve, dust powdered sugar on top.

Instant Pot Salted Caramel Cheesecake

Total Preparation & Cook Time: 50 minutes

Servings – 6

Nutritional info: Calories: 3065, Fats: 220g, Carbs: 225g, Protein: 51g, Fiber: 1.7g, Sugar: 96.6g

Ingredients:
Crust:

- 1½ cups finely crushed graham crackers,

- 4 tbsp butter, melted

- 2 tbsp sugar

Cheesecake:

- 2 boxes of cream cheese

- ¼ cup sour cream

- 1 tbsp flour

- ½ tsp salt

- 1½ tsp vanilla

- 2 eggs

- 2/3 cups brown sugar

Topping:

- ½ cup caramel sauce

- 1 tsp flaked sea salt

Directions:

1. Prepare a springform pan, 7 inches, for baking.

2. To prepare crust, combine well the crumbs, butter and sugar then press into of bottom and sides of pan evenly with an offset- spatula.

3. Combine the sugar and the cream cheese in a stand mixer and mix well until combined. Mix in sour cream and beat for another 30 seconds still smooth consistency. Next, add in salt, flour, and vanilla and mix about 10 seconds. Combine eggs and mix till smooth. Do not over scrape.

4. Pour cheese mixture into prepare crust.

5. In the instant pot, fill the bottom with 2 cups water and place trivet.

6. Cover pan with foil and create foil sling to place springform pan inside the pan. Secure lid and valve and press Manual. Adjust to cook on high pressure for 35 minutes.

7. Once cook is done, open pot to allow pressure to release naturally.

8. Remove pan using sling and place on wire rack to cool.

9. Cover cheesecake with cling wrap and place in the fridge to chill for 4 hours. To serve, cut cheesecake into slices and serve with a drizzle of caramel sauce and sprinkle of sea salt.

Instant Pot Zesty Key Lime Pie

Total Preparation & Cook Time: 50 minutes

Servings – 6

Nutritional info: Calories: 1911, Fats: 128.2g, Carbs: 137g, Protein: 23.6g, Fiber: 3.6g, Sugar: 104.2g

Ingredients:

Crust:

- 2/3 digestive biscuit crumbs

- 3 tbsp unsalted butter, melted

- 1 tbsp sugar

Filling:

- 4 egg yolks

- ⅓ cup sour cream

- 2 tbsp grated key lime zest

- 1 can of condensed milk (sweetened)

- ⅓ cup lime juice

Directions:

1. Prepare a springform pan for baking.

2. In a large mixing bowl, make the crust by combining the crumbs along with the butter and the sugar. Using an off-set spatula press the crust into place. Place in fridge to set.

3. Meanwhile, make pie by beating egg yolks till light yellow color.

4. Slowly stir in sweetened condensed milk until thick consistency.

5. Mix in lime juice gradually and beat mixture till smooth.

6. Combine the zest and the sour cream before adding it to the rest of the mixture

7. Fill the crust with the batter and cover pan with foil.

8. Pour in 1 cup of water into Instant Pot and create foil sling to center and place pan into a trivet.

9. Lock the lid and close the valve. Cook on high pressure for 15 minutes.

10. Once the timer goes off, naturally release pressure for 10 minutes after turning pot off.

11. Perform quick release again to remove any leftover steam. Remove lid when valve drops.

12. Remove cheesecake and give it the time it needs to thoroughly cool.

13. Once cooled, cover cheesecake again with cling wrap and refrigerated for 4 hours or overnight to chill.

14. Cut chilled cake into sliced, top with whipped cream and grated lime zest to serve.

Instant Pot Banana Pumpkin Bundt Cake

Total Preparation & Cook Time: 50 minutes

Servings – 6

Nutritional info: Calories: 1782, Fats: 45.1g, Carbs: 322g, Protein: 27g,

Fiber: 8.0g, Sugar: 175g

Ingredients:

- 2/3 tsp pumpkin pie spice
- ½ tsp baking powder
- Salt, 1 pinch
- 1 large egg
- ¼ cup Greek yogurt
- 15 oz can 100% pureed pumpkin
- 1 tsp baking soda
- 2/3 cup whole wheat flour
- 2 tbsp canola oil
- 2/3 cup flour
- 1 medium banana mashed
- 2/3 cup dark chocolate chips or chocolate chunks
- ⅓ tsp vanilla
- ¾ cup sugar

Directions:

1. Combine the baking soda and flour with the salt along with the pumpkin pie spice and set aside.

2. With an electric mixer, mix banana, oil, yogurt, sugar, pureed pumpkin, vanilla, and egg.

3. Keep mixer on low and gradually add in the dry ingredients till well incorporated.

4. Add the chips.

5. Add the results in the previously prepared pan. Bang pan to release air.

6. Use paper towels and foil to cover bundt pan and wrap foil around the bottom.

7. Pour 1 ½ cups of water into the inner pot and place trivet with handles inside.

8. Place bundt pans on top of the trivet. Close and lock the lid.

9. Click on Manual and set to cook for 35 minutes.

10. Allow pressure to release for 10 minutes after cooking is done then release valve and remove the lid.

11. Remove pan and leave to ensure it has plenty of time to properly cool.

12. Once cooled, used a spatula to go around the sides of the pan to release cake.

Instant Pot Pecan Pumpkin Pie

Total Preparation & Cook Time: 4 Hours

Servings – 6

Nutritional info: Calories: 741, Fats: 21.2g, Carbs: 127g, Protein: 19.4g,

Fiber: 11g, Sugar: 89g

Ingredients:

Crust:

- ½ cup crushed spiced cookies

- ⅓ cup toasted pecans, chopped

- 2 tbsp butter melted

Filling:

- ½ cup evaporated milk

- ½ cup light brown sugar

- 1 ½ cups pumpkin

- 1 ½ tsp pumpkin pie spice

- ½ tsp salt

- 1 egg, beaten

Directions:

1. Prepare your springform pan

2. Combine the cookie crumbs, pecans, and butter.

3. Spread evenly to the sides. Freeze for 10 minutes.

4. Meanwhile, make the filling. Mix salt, sugar and

pumpkin pie spice.

5. Add in the remaining ingredients and add the results to the prepared crust.

6. Cover pan with aluminum foil.

7. In the Instant pot, pour 1 cup water and place a trivet with handles to the bottom. Carefully place pan on top of the trivet.

8. Lock and close the lid. Select High Pressure and cook for 35 minutes.

9. When the timer starts beeping, turn off the pressure cooker and allow for natural pressure release.

10. Do a quick pressure release to let go of any remaining pressure then remove the lid.

11. To a doneness test to the middle of the pie. If the pie is not set, then cook for another 5 minutes.

12. Once done, remove the pan and the foil and let everything cool.

13. When it has cooled, place it in the fridge covered with plastic. Allow to chill for 4 hours.

14. To serve, slice pie and serve with freshly whipped cream.

Creamy Instant Pot Egg Custard

Total Preparation & Cook Time: 12 minutes

Servings – 6

Nutritional info: Calories: 1442, Fats: 36g, Carbs: 210g, Protein: 62.5,

Fiber: 0g, Sugar: 196g

Ingredients:

- 6 eggs beaten
- ¼ tsp cinnamon
- 1 tsp vanilla extract
- Pinch of salt
- ¾ cup sugar
- Garnish
- Sprinkle of nutmeg
- Chopped fresh fruit
- Sprinkle of cinnamon
- 3 ½ cups milk

Directions:

1. Combine the eggs, vanilla, milk salt and sugar and blend until thoroughly combined but not over mix.

2. Add the results to the pressure cooker safe bowl before covering it using foil. Create venting holes.

3. Add in the water and add a trivet with handles to the bottom.

4. Insert the bowl on top of the trivet.

5. Close and lock the lid of the cooker and close the valve too. Cook on high pressure for 7 minutes.

6. Once cooking is done, the pot will beep and allow at least 10 minutes for the pressure to release naturally.

7. To serve, top custard with either fresh fruits or berries and sprinkle with nutmeg or cinnamon.

Chocolaty Brownie Instant Pot Cake

Total Preparation & Cook Time: 30 minutes

Servings – 6

Nutritional info: Calories: 989, Fats: 88.9g, Carbs: 17g, Protein: 23.4g,

Fiber: 8.8g, Sugar: 27.4g

Ingredients:

- 4 tbsp cocoa powder
- 2 tbsp powdered sugar
- 4 tbsp unsalted butter
- 2 tbsp chocolate chips
- ¼ tsp vanilla extract
- ⅔ cup sugar
- ½ cup flour
- 2 eggs

Directions:

1. Microwave butter and chocolate chips in a microwave-safe bowl for 1 minute.

2. In another mixing bowl, beat the butter and sugar until well combined. Fold in the chocolate chips. Pour in the vanilla and eggs and beat again until well blended.

3. Sift the flour and cocoa over the wet ingredients and mix until well combined.

4. Place trivet inside the Instant Pot and add 1 cup of water.

5. Grease ramekins and pour the batter into them, leaving half an inch to allow dough to rise.

6. Cover ramekins with foil.

7. Set to cook on high pressure for 18 minutes.

8. Once done, perform quick release and set brownies to cool.

9. Once ramekins have cooled, sprinkle powdered sugar to serve.

Chapter 5 - Vegan & Vegetarian

Kamut, Arugula and Orange Quinoa Salad

Total Preparation & Cook Time: 40 minutes

Servings – 6

Nutritional info: Calories: 127, Fats: 8.6g, Carbs: 11.7g, Protein: 2.8g, Fiber: 2.1g, Sugar: 0.04g

Ingredients:

- ½ cup shelled walnuts, roughly chopped
- 1 cup whole Kamut grains
- 1 bunch rocket arugula
- ½ cup Pecorino Romano cheese ribbons
- ½ lemon juice
- 1 tsp vegetable oil
- 2 cups water
- 1 tsp salt
- 2 medium blood oranges, peeled, sliced cross-wise
- 1 tbsp cold-pressed extra virgin olive oil

Directions:

1. In a large bowl, place Kamut in bowl with 4 cups water and ½ lemon juice. Soak overnight.
2. Rinse and strain Kamut just before using.
3. In the Instant Pot, add in strained Kamut together with

salt, vegetable oil and 2 cups water.

4. Close and lock lid and cook on high till pot reaches pressure, then lower the heat to maintain least amount of pressure. Cook for 15 minutes.

5. When beeper goes off, naturally release steam and open pot. Allow pressure to come down.

6. In a serving bowl combine Kamut, arugula, orange pieces, walnuts and olive oil.

7. Combine all ingredients and drizzle Pecorino Romano ribbons.

Instant Pot Refried Beans

Total Preparation & Cook Time: 40 minutes

Servings – 6

Nutritional info: Calories: 1000, Fats: 10.5g, Carbs: 274g, Protein: 88.7g, Fiber: 67.5g, Sugar: 19.1g

Ingredients:

- 2 cups dried pinto beans
- 1 large onion, cut into quarters
- 4 cloves garlic, peeled and roughly chopped
- 1 jalapeno - seeded
- 1 tsp salt
- ½ tsp black pepper
- 1 tsp paprika
- 1 tsp cumin
- 1 tsp chili powder
- ½ cup salsa
- Cilantro - to taste
- 3 cups low sodium vegetable broth

Directions:

1. Rinse pinto beans.
2. Place all ingredients into the Instant Pot and stir to combine.
3. Close the lid and seal the steam valve.

4. Click Manual and adjust cooking time to 28 minutes.

5. Once beeper goes off, leave pot for 10 minutes and then turn the valve to release remaining steal.

6. Open lid and stir contents well.

7. You can either blend the beans or mash it to achieve desired consistency.

8. Serve warm.

Healthy Coconut Almond Risotto

Total Preparation & Cook Time: 35 minutes

Servings – 4

Nutritional info: Calories: 888, Fats: 57.2g, Carbs: 101g, Protein: 5.5g, Fiber: 5.3g, Sugar: 8g

Ingredients:

- 2 cups vanilla almond milk
- 1 cup organic regular coconut milk
- 1 cup risotto rice of choice
- 1½–2 tsp vanilla extract
- ¼ cup toasted coconut flakes
- 1/3 cup agave syrup, or more to taste

Directions:

1. In your Instant Pot, click 'Sauté' and add the coconut and almond milk.
2. Stir constantly and bring to a boil. Add the rice and stir to combine.
3. Close the Instant Pot lid and seal the valve.
4. Click on 'Manual' and adjust cooking time to reduce to 5 minutes.
5. Once the timer goes off, allow the natural release of pressure and then turn off valve to remove remaining pressure.
6. Next, add in vanilla extract and agave syrup. Stir well.
7. Place risotto on service dish and top up with toasted coconut flakes and sliced almonds.

Fluffy Paleo Banana Bread

Total Preparation & Cook Time: 50 Minutes

Servings – 8

Nutritional info: Calories: 200, Fats: 18.1g, Carbs: 19.4g, Protein: 6.4g, Fiber: 3.2g, Sugar: 12.1g

Ingredients:

- 1 egg
- ⅓ cup softened coconut oil
- ¾ cup coconut sugar
- 1 tsp vanilla
- 1 ½ tsp cream of tartar
- 2 ripe bananas, mashed
- ½ tsp baking soda
- 1 ½ cup cassava flour
- 1 tsp baking powder
- Pinch of salt
- ⅓ cup coconut milk

Directions:

1. In a bowl, make buttermilk by combining cream of tartar together with coconut milk. Set aside.

2. Cream together sugar and butter and add in egg together with vanilla extract. Stir well. Add mashed bananas and stir well to combine

3. In a separate bowl, mix cassava flour, baking soda,

baking powder and salt. Gradually pour dry ingredients and blend wet ingredients and mix well to combine

4. Add in buttermilk mixture and cover with foil.

5. Using a seven-inch cake pan, pour in the mixture

6. In the Instant Cooker pot, add in 2 cups of water and set the metal trivet rack at the bottom of the Instant Pot.

7. Lower your cake pan to the trivet, close the lid and seal the pot

8. Press 'Manual' to 30 minutes cook time.

9. When the timer goes off, allow it to naturally release pressure, about 15 minutes.

10. Once the pressure is gone, remove the link and lift the trivet and pan.

11. Remove the foil and allow your cake to cool in the pan.

12. The cake will quickly come off the pan once it has completely cooled.

Indian Red Curry Lentil

Total Preparation & Cook Time: 30 minutes

Servings – 6

Nutritional info: Calories: 350, Fats: 22g, Carbs: 35g, Protein: 67g, Fiber: 212g, Sugar: 0.7g

Ingredients:

- 1 can organic coconut milk
- 1 oz crushed tomatoes
- 2 cups dry red lentils
- 3 tbsp tomato paste
- ½ onion diced
- 4 cloves garlic, roughly minced
- 1 tbsp fresh ginger, peeled and roughly minced
- 2 tsp vegetable bouillon
- 5 cups water
- 2 ½ tbsp curry powder
- 1 tsp smoked paprika
- ½ tsp cayenne powder
- 1 cup fresh spinach, chopped

Directions:

1. Set cooker to 'Sauté' and sauté onions, garlic, and ginger for 4 minutes
2. Add remaining ingredients except for spinach until the

curry is done with cooking. You should see the oil break to the surface

3. Place lid and secure, closing the valve.

4. Set 'Manual' button to 15 minutes cook time.

5. Once the timer goes off, let the pressure release naturally, 10 minutes.

6. Remove lid and add spinach. Stir to wilt.

7. Serve warm with cooked rice or naan or Bread.

Vegan One Pot Pasta

Total Preparation & Cook Time: 20 minutes

Servings – 4

Nutritional info: Calories: 139, Fats: 25g, Carbs: 44g, Protein: 35.7g, Fiber: 22.8g, Sugar: 3.2g

Ingredients:

- ½ lb red lentil pasta
- 1 ½ cups cooked chickpeas
- 2 ½ organic vegetable broth
- 1 cup organic cherry tomatoes, halved
- 1 small organic red onion sliced thinly
- 2 bell peppers, sliced thinly
- ½ tsp miso
- ½ tsp pepper
- ½ tsp red pepper flakes
- 4 big fresh basil leaves, torn
- 2 lemon slices
- 4 garlic cloves, mashed
- 1 cup baby spinach
- 1 cup broccoli, cut into florets
- 1 cup carrots, julienned

Directions:

1. Turn on your pot and set to 'Sauté.'

2. When pot becomes slightly hot, add in your vegetables, seasoning, and pasta. Stir to combine. Cook for 8 minutes and allow pressure to reduce and release naturally.

3. Add in a handful of spinach when the pressure has reduced and allow heat to wilt the spinach.

4. Dish out pasta into serving the dish and spread some parmesan cheese as garnish.

Instant Pot Potatoes & Chickpeas Curry

Total Preparation & Cook Time: 1 Hour

Servings – 4

Nutritional info: Calories: 1120, Fats: 1.1g, Carbs: 27g, Protein: 5.5g, Fiber: 5.4g, Sugar: 12.2g

Ingredients:

- 2 cups chickpeas- soaked overnight
- 2 tea bags
- 4 small pieces of Indian gooseberry
- 2 black cardamoms
- Whole spices
- Dry spices
- 1 tsp cumin seeds
- 2 small bay leaves
- 1 small cinnamon stick
- 4 cloves
- 1 tsp salt
- ½ tsp red chili
- 1 tsp garam masala & 1 tsp coriander powder
- 2 tsp chana masala
- Ginger garlic paste
- ½ inch ginger
- 5 cloves garlic
- 1 big onion thinly sliced

- 2 medium sized potatoes, finely chopped
- 1 cup tomato puree

Directions:

1. Add your pre-soaked chickpeas into the Instant Pot and pour in another 2 cups of water together with the Indian gooseberries and tea bags.

2. Close and lock the lid to your Instant Pot. Select Manual and reduce the timber to cook for 15 minutes.

3. Once the cooking is done, allow the steam to release gradually. Remove chickpeas and the flavored water. Reserve water.

4. Clean and dry the pot then switch it on to Sauté mode.

5. Pour in the oil and bloom the cumin seeds, cinnamon, cloves and cumin seeds.

6. Once the seeds start to bloom, add the onions and fry. Then add the garlic and ginger paste. Fry for a few more minutes till fragrant.

7. Toss in the chopped potatoes and stir to combine. Sauté potatoes till sides start to brown.

8. Pour the tomato puree in and mix well. Sauté till the oil breaks.

9. Add in your spices together with one tbsp of oil.

10. Toss in the cooked chickpeas and mix well. To this, add 3 cups of the cooked water.

11. Close the lid, click on Manual and cook on high pressure for 15 minutes.

12. Once cooking time is done, remove chickpeas and place on serving dish. Garnish with chopped parsley.

Instant Pot Vegan Lasagna Soup

Total Preparation & Cook Time: 4 Hour 15 minutes

Servings – 6

Nutritional info: Calories: 1494, Fats: 90.3g, Carbs: 119g, Protein: 71.2g, Fiber: 29g, Sugar: 32g

Ingredients:

For the Soup:

- 4 ½ cups vegetable broth
- 1 medium onion diced
- 3 garlic cloves, minced
- ¾ cup dried brown lentils
- 1 tsp dried basil
- 1 tsp dried oregano
- 14 oz. can dice tomatoes
- 14 oz. can crush tomatoes
- 8 lasagna noodles, broken into pieces
- 3 cups chopped spinach leaves

For the Ricotta:

- 1 cup raw cashews, soaked, drained and rinsed
- ¼ cup almond milk
- ¼ lb extra firm tofu, drained
- 3 to 4 tbsp prepared vegan pesto
- 1 tbsp lemon juice

- Salt and pepper to taste

Directions:

1. To make the Lasagna Soup:

2. Into the Instant pot, toss in onions and garlic, basil, oregano, lentils and pour in the broth. Stir everything together to combine. Click Manual and set timber to 1 hour.

3. Cook lentils till it is slightly firm, about 1 hour.

4. Next, add in the tomatoes and stir to combine. Cook on high pressure again for another 30 minutes.

5. Add in the spinach as well as the lasagna noodles. Mix everything and cook another 30 minutes till spinach has wilted and noodles are al dente.

6. Season soup with pepper and salt.

7. To make the Pesto Ricotta:

8. Blend cashews and milk together in a food processor. Add in the tofu and pulse till you get a ricotta kind of mixture. Combine pesto, lemon juice and then add a dash of salt and pepper to season.

9. To serve, divide soup between bowls and place your vegan ricotta pesto.

Polenta in the Instant Pot

Total Preparation & Cook Time: 30 minutes

Servings – 6

Nutritional info: Calories: 189, Fats: 7.5g, Carbs: 9.3g, Protein: 20.6g, Fiber: 3.4g, Sugar: 2.7g

Ingredients:

- 4 cups vegetable broth
- 1 cup polenta
- ½ tsp salt
- ¼ cup of fresh herbs, roughly chopped
- 2 tsp Italian seasoning

Directions:

1. To the Instant pot, add the brother and season with Italian seasoning. Whisk and then add in the polenta and salt.

2. Set valve to seal, close and lock lid. Select 'Porridge' and adjust Pot to cook at 5 minutes.

3. When cooking is done, allow the polenta to rest inside the pot for 10 minutes.

4. Press Cancel and open the Pot. Turn the valve to vent and allow pressure to release.

5. Whisk in the polenta and check for seasoning.

6. Add in herbs as well as cheese if you like.

7. Serve polenta warm.

Vegan Lentil Bolognese in an Instant Pot

Total Preparation & Cook Time: 25 Minutes

Servings – 4

Nutritional info: Calories: 363, Fats: 9.5g, Carbs: 67g, Protein: 11.4g, Fiber: 14.2g, Sugar: 37g

Ingredients:

- 1 cup of black lentils, washed
- 28 oz. can of fire roasted chopped tomatoes
- 1 yellow onion diced
- 4 cloves of garlic, minced
- 3 medium carrots diced
- 1 can of tomato paste
- 4 cups of water
- 2 tbsp of Italian seasoning, dry
- Red pepper flakes to taste
- Salt and pepper
- Balsamic vinegar

Directions:

1. Add water and boil your pasta until al dente. Remove and set aside.

2. Combine all your ingredients into the Instant Pot again and set to manual for 15 minutes cook time. Make sure to close the steam release valve.

3. When cooking is done, allow for natural pressure

release.

4. Once the steam has done, open your pot and pour in a healthy dose of balsamic vinegar.

5. Season with salt and pepper.

6. Ladle the sauce over the pasta and garnish with fresh chopped parsley.

Instant Pot Mac & Cheese

Total Preparation & Cook Time: 15 Minutes

Servings – 4

Nutritional info: Calories: 53, Fats: 3.5g, Carbs: 4g, Protein: 2.8g, Fiber: 1.7g, Sugar: 0.8g

Ingredients:

- 1 box elbow macaroni
- cups water
- 1 tbsp mustard
- 1 tsp hot sauce
- 1 tsp salt
- 1 heaping tbsp of Earth Balance
- 1 bag vegan cheddar shreds
- 1 cup plain unsweetened almond milk

Directions:

1. Pour the water into your Instant Pot. Then, toss in your macaroni, mustard, hot sauce, salt and earth balance. Give it a good stir once then press Manual and leave to cook for 4 minutes.

2. When the timer beeps, release the pressure off the pot and give the macaroni another stir.

3. Add in the vegan cheddar and milk. Stir to combine.

4. Close the lid back on and allow the pasta to rest on Warm mode till it's time to eat.

5. Serve with fresh or dried parsley.

Instant Pot Cranberry Vegan Cake

Total Preparation & Cook Time: 45 minutes

Servings – 4

Nutritional info: Calories: 203, Fats: 4.7g, Carbs: 35g, Protein: 4.4g, Fiber: 11g, Sugar: 17g

Ingredients:
Dry Ingredients:

- 1¼ cup whole wheat pastry flour

- ½ tsp ground cardamom

- ½ tsp baking soda

- ½ tsp baking powder

- ⅛ tsp salt

Wet Ingredients:

- ½ cup unsweetened almond milk

- ¼ cup agave sweetener

- 2 tbsp ground flax seeds

- 2 tbsp mild oil

Additional:

- 1 cup chopped pear

- ½ cup chopped fresh cranberries

For Cooking:

- 1½ cups water

Directions:

1. Use a 7-inch bundt pan and prepare it by oiling it. Set aside.

2. In a mixing bowl, combine all your dry ingredients.

3. In a separate bowl, mix all your wet ingredients.

4. Slowly add the wet to the dry ingredients and carefully fold in the chopped pear and cranberries.

5. Spread this mixture evenly into your pan and cover it with foil.

6. Insert a trivet into the Instant pot and add water to it.

7. Place bundt pan into the pot and close and lock lid. Close valve and cook on high pressure for 35 minutes. Once done, allow pressure to release naturally.

8. Once done, remove the lid and lit pan out. Remove foil.

9. Allow the cake to cool in the bundt pan before removing and serving.

Instant Pot Vegan Posole

Total Preparation & Cook Time: 35 Minutes

Servings – 6

Nutritional info: Calories: 2571, Fats: 37.9g, Carbs: 498g, Protein: 69g, Fiber: 56g, Sugar: 34g

Ingredients:

- 14 oz. red chili puree
- 25 oz. can hominy
- 1 medium onion
- 8 garlic cloves
- 1 tbsp oil
- 2 20 oz cans of jackfruit
- 6 cups vegetable broth
- Garnishes: lime juice, oregano, red pepper flakes, cilantro, shredded cabbage, and thinly sliced radishes.

Directions:

1. Turn on your Instant Pot and click Sauté. Add in oil and sauté your onions and garlic for 5 minutes.

2. Add in your chili puree and cook till the oil breaks.

3. Add in your jackfruit and cook till it is slightly tender.

4. Then, use a masher to mash the jackfruit to your desired consistency. To this, add in the vegetable brother.

5. Click Manual on the pot then lock and close the lid.

Cook on high pressure for 10 minutes.

6. Once done, allow the pot to go on natural pressure release.

7. Remove lid, add in the hominy and then cook again for 1 minute.

8. Again, allow for natural pressure release and season with black pepper and salt.

9. To serve, place posole on serving dish and garnish with lime juice and a sprinkling of oregano and red pepper flakes. You can also add shredded cabbage, sliced radishes, and chopped oregano.

Vegan Mushroom Risotto

Total Preparation & Cook Time: 15 Minutes

Servings – 6

Nutritional info: Calories: 925, Fats: 16.8g, Carbs: 17g, Protein: 23g, Fiber: 12.3g, Sugar: 3.2g

Ingredients:

- ½ cup minced white onion
- 3 cloves minced garlic
- 1 tbsp olive oil
- 4 oz mushrooms, chopped
- 1 tsp salt
- 1 tsp thyme
- ½ cup dry white wine
- 3 cups vegetable broth
- 1 cup risotto rice
- ¼ cup lemon juice
- 2 cups fresh spinach
- 1 tbsp vegan butter
- 1 ½ tbsp nutritional yeast
- Black pepper, to taste

Directions:

1. Turn on your pot and click the Sauté feature. Add in the oil and sauté the onions and garlic till fragrant.

2. Toss in your rice and stir to combine. Next, pour in the broth, wine, thyme, mushrooms and season with salt.

3. Close the lid and switch the valve to 'Seal.' Click on Manual and reduce cooking time to 5 minutes.

4. When cooking time is up, perform quick release and carefully open your Instant Pot lid.

5. To this, add the yeast, butter, spinach and season with black pepper. Stir everything well. If it is too liquid, then allow risotto to sit in the pot for a couple of minutes to thicken.

Chapter 6 - Soups, Stews and Chowders

Instant Pot Stuffed Pepper Soup

Total Preparation & Cook Time: 20 minutes

Servings – 4

Nutritional info: Calories: 1343, Fats: 20g, Carbs: 238g, Protein: 68.7g, Fiber: 66.8g, Sugar: 59g

Ingredients:

- 1 tbsp extra virgin olive oil
- 3-4 cloves garlic, minced
- ½ onion, thinly sliced
- ½ can tomato paste
- 1 tsp cumin
- 1 tsp chili powder
- 1 tsp black pepper
- 1 tsp salt
- 2 bell peppers, any color, sliced or diced
- ½-1 lb. ground beef, uncooked
- 14.5 oz can tomatoes
- 5 cup beef broth
- 1 cup organic brown rice, uncooked
- 3 tbsp cornmeal
- Parmesan cheese, for garnish

- Green onions, for garnish

Directions:

1. Click on 'Sauté' on the Instant Pot. Add in the uncooked ground beef and brown slightly 5 minutes.

2. Toss in garlic and onions and sauté till ground beef is cooked through, and onions are translucent.

3. Turn Sauté function off and stir in tomato paste. Add cumin, salt, and black pepper. Stir to combine.

4. Add in peppers, beef broth and diced tomatoes. Mix well.

5. Combine rice and mix till well blended.

6. Put the lid on the Instant pot, close the valve and click Manual to cook on high pressure for 23 minutes.

7. Once beeper goes off, release pressure immediately and turn off the pot.

8. Little by little, add the cornmeal and stir well, so it doesn't clump.

9. Serve soup warm garnished with parmesan cheese and fresh dinner rolls.

Instant Pot Gluten Free Minestrone Soup

Total Preparation & Cook Time: 18 minutes

Servings – 6

Nutritional info: Calories: 1980, Fats: 20g, Carbs: 217g, Protein: 124g, Fiber: 112g, Sugar: 23g

Ingredients:

- 2 tbsp lard or olive oil
- 2 stalks celery, diced
- 1 large onion diced
- 1 large carrot diced
- 3 cloves garlic, minced
- 1 tsp dried oregano
- 1 tsp dried basil
- Sea salt and pepper, to taste
- 28 oz. can tomatoes
- 2 cups freshly cooked, drained white beans
- 4 cups vegetable broth
- 1 bay leaf
- ½ cup fresh spinach, torn to shreds
- 1 cup gluten-free elbow pasta
- ⅓ cup finely grated parmesan cheese
- 1-2 tbsp fresh pesto

Directions:

1. Click sauté on Instant Pot. Once the pot is slightly hot, pour in olive oil and toss in carrots, onions, garlic, and celery. Cook till softened.

2. Toss in oregano, basil, salt and pepper to taste.

3. Pulse tomatoes with its liquid in a food processor and processed till tomatoes are diced.

4. Add in tomatoes, broth, spinach, pasta and bay leaf.

5. Close the Instant Pot lid and set to Manual and cook on high pressure for 6 minutes.

6. When the pot reaches pressure, let it cook for another 6 minutes.

7. When the timer goes off, let sit for 2 minutes. The quick release to let go of steam.

8. Remove lid then add white beans.

9. To serve, load soup in serving bowls and top with parmesan cheese and some pesto.

Beef Lentil Instant Pot Stew

Total Preparation & Cook Time: 18 minutes

Servings – 6

Nutritional info: Calories: 2224, Fats: 36g, Carbs: 253g, Protein: 217g, Fiber: 84g, Sugar: 29g

Ingredients:

- 4 tbsp brown gravy mix
- 1 lb beef, cut into small cubes
- 1 cup dry lentils
- 1 onion diced
- 2-4 potatoes, peeled and diced
- 1 cup carrots, diced
- 5 cloves of garlic, minced
- 4 cups beef stock
- 1 can dice tomatoes, with juice
- Salt and pepper, to taste

Directions:

1. Make sure your beef cubes are slightly smaller than your potato cubes so that its cooks entirely in the same amount of time.

2. In your Instant Pot, toss in your chopped onions, garlic, beef, carrots, and potatoes.

3. Wash and rinse your lentils then add them into the pot together with your canned tomatoes, beef stock, and

gravy mix.

4. Set your Instant Pot to 20 minutes cook time and walk away.

5. When the beeper goes off, allow for natural pressure release.

6. Serve soup with sliced green onions.

Creamy Corn Instant Pot Chowder

Total Preparation & Cook Time: 15 minutes

Servings – 6

Nutritional info: Calories: 2500, Fats: 45g, Carbs: 289g, Protein: 60.7g, Fiber: 27.3g, Sugar: 38.6g

Ingredients:

- 4 slices bacon, cooked and diced
- 6 ears fresh corn, shucked
- 4 tbsp butter
- ½ cup chopped onion
- 3 cups water
- 2 medium potatoes diced
- 2 tbsp cornstarch
- 2 tbsp water
- 3 cups half-and-half
- ⅛ tsp ground cayenne
- 2 tbsp fresh parsley
- Salt and freshly ground black pepper

Directions:

1. On your Instant Pot, Select Sauté and add the butter to the pot. Once the butter has melted, toss in the onions and cook until tender.

2. Add in 3 cups of water to the pot, lock the lid and cook on high pressure for 10 minutes.

3. When the pot beeps, turn off the pressure and perform the quick release.

4. Remove the corn cobs from the pot and leave only the broth.

5. Place a steamer basket in the pressure cooker and add in diced potatoes as well as corn kernels.

6. Close and lock lid and proceed to cook on high pressure for 4 minutes.

7. When the timer starts beeping, turn off the cooker and perform the quick release. Once the steam has gone, remove steamer basket.

8. Next, dissolve cornstarch in 2 tbsp water. In your Instant Pot, Select Simmer and add cornstarch mixture into pot and stir till mixture thickens.

9. To this mixture, add in milk, cayenne pepper, diced potatoes, corn kernels, parsley, and bacon. Add salt and pepper.

10. Simmer soup on low but does not bring to boil.

11. Serve in bowls and garnish with chopped parsley.

Instant Pot Oxtail Stew

Total Preparation & Cook Time: 2 hours

Servings – 4

Nutritional info: Calories: 658, Fats: 29g, Carbs: 56g, Protein: 55g, Fiber: 10g, Sugar: 25g

Ingredients:

- 1 kg oxtail pieces, fat trimmed
- 6 cloves of garlic, chopped
- 1 medium onion, chopped
- 2 medium leeks, sliced thinly
- 3 ribs of celery, chopped
- 4 small carrots cut into 1-inch chunks
- 2 sprigs of rosemary, sprigs of parsley, and sprigs of thyme
- 2 cans of diced tomatoes
- 1 cup red wine
- 1 cup chicken stock
- 1 tbsp tomato paste
- 2 tbsp Worcestershire sauce
- 1 tbsp balsamic vinegar
- ½ tsp salt for sauce and 2 tsp salts for meat
- 2 tsp ground black pepper
- ½ tsp ground allspice

- 2 tbsp of parsley, chopped

- 2 tbsp olive oil

- 1 tsp xantham gum

Directions:

1. Using a kitchen twine, tie the thyme, parsley and rosemary in a bunch

2. Marinade the oxtail pieces with salt, pepper and ground pepper

3. Click Sauté on the Instant Pot and pour in olive oil.

4. Sauté oxtail pieces till browned on all sides. Remove from pot and set aside.

5. In the same pot, sauté garlic, leek, onions and celery till slightly caramelized.

6. Pour into the pot the wine, balsamic vinegar, chicken stock and tomatoes and tomato paste. Add in the herb bundle and allow mixture to simmer for 5 minutes. Stir occasionally, ensuring the browned bits are dislodged from the bottom of the pot.

7. Place oxtail pieces back into stew, immersing all pieces.

8. Click 'Meat' on Instant Pot. This will cook the meat for 35 minutes. When the timer goes off, allow for natural pressure release.

9. Add in carrots into the pot and click Manual to cook on high pressure for 10 minutes. Allow for natural pressure release again.

10. Remove oxtail and carrots and place on a dish. Set the post again on Sauté mode and sauté for another 10 minutes till the stew has reduced.

11. Toss in the xantham gum and stir to combine. Reduce sauce for at least 10 minutes.

12. To serve, pour stew over oxtail and carrots and garnish with chopped parsley.

Instant Pot Dumplings & Chicken Soup

Total Preparation & Cook Time: 20 minutes

Servings – 4

Nutritional info: Calories: 2622, Fats: 205g, Carbs: 36g, Protein: 7g, Fiber: 1.5g, Sugar: 7.6g

Ingredients:

- 1 lb chicken breast, cubed
- 2 cups cubed potatoes
- 1 small diced onion
- 3 cups chicken broth
- 1 cup heavy cream
- 16oz bag frozen mixed veggies
- 16oz cheddar cheese
- 2 tbsp corn starch

For Dumplings:

- 2 cups Bisquick
- 2/3 cup milk

Directions:

1. Turn on the Instant Pot and toss in chicken breast, potatoes and your mixed veggies.

2. Pour the broth into the pot and set to cook on Manual on high pressure for 15 minutes.

3. Perform quick release then turn off and on pot and switch to sauté. Whisk in your cornstarch and heavy

cream and bring mixture to a boil. Toss in the cheese.

4. Allow mixture to come to a slight boil.

5. In the meantime, mix together the Bisquick and milk. Drop in spoonfuls of this mixture into your pot.

6. Cover the pot with the lid and allow dumplings to cook in the broth till the dumplings rise to the top- which means it's cooked.

7. Serve hot.

Asian Thai Coconut Chicken Soup

Total Preparation & Cook Time: 10 minutes

Servings – 6

Nutritional info: Calories: 2745, Fats: 150g, Carbs: 56g, Protein: 222g, Fiber: 3.5g, Sugar: 30g

Ingredients:

- 2 tbsp oil

- 1 small onion quartered

- 2 lb boneless chicken breast, skin, removed, cut into cubes

- 2 tbsp Thai red curry paste

- 1 red bell pepper cut into strips

- 6 slices galangal

- 6 kaffir lime leaves, roughly chopped

- 3 cups chicken broth

- 2 tbsp fish sauce

- 1 heaping tbsp sugar

- ¾ cup coconut milk

- 2 ½ tbsp lime juice

- Cilantro leaves

Directions:

1. Turn on your Instant Pot and click on Sauté. When the pot heats up, add in your oil and sauté onions for 10

seconds then add in the chicken cubes.

2. Sauté till the chicken surface is white then pour in the Thai curry paste, galangal, bell peppers, kaffir lime leaves and stir all to combine well.

3. Add the chicken broth and fish sauce and season to taste with sugar.

4. Select high pressure, close the pot and cook for 10 minutes.

5. Perform quick release when the pot begins to beep.

6. Once the valve drops, remove the lid and stir in the coconut milk and lime juice. Mix well.

7. Serve broth warm with a side of steamed rice.

Refreshing Summer Squash Soup
with Coconut Milk

Total Preparation & Cook Time: 20 minutes

Servings – 6

Nutritional info: Calories: 191, Fats: 5.6g, Carbs: 15g, Protein: 18.9g, Fiber: 2.9g, Sugar: 5.6g

Ingredients:

- 4 yellow squash, roughly chopped or sliced
- 1 small onion, chopped
- 4 cloves garlic, chopped
- ½ cup full fat coconut milk
- 4 cups vegetable broth
- ½ tsp salt
- ¼ tsp pepper
- 1 ½ tsp curry powder
- ½ tsp cumin
- For garnish: basil, or fresh croutons.

Directions:

1. Into your Instant pot, toss in squash, onions and garlic and sprinkle in the curry powder, cumin, pepper and salt.

2. Pour in your brother until it just about covers the vegetables.

3. Put the lid on and press Manual to cook on High

Temperature for 10 minutes.

4. When the cooking is done, release the pressure manually and then use an immersion blender to blend the mixture inside the pot.

5. After this, pour in the coconut milk, salt and season with pepper.

6. Serve soup with sourdough bread and drizzle with a little coconut milk for garnish.

Instant Pot Mexican Albondigas Soup

Total Preparation & Cook Time: 30 minutes

Servings – 6

Nutritional info: Calories: 1956, Fats: 75.6g, Carbs: 153g, Protein: 174.9g, Fiber: 15.9g, Sugar: 21g

Ingredients:

Meatballs:

- 1 lb lean ground beef
- 2 cloves garlic, chopped
- ½ onion, sliced
- ½ green bell pepper, chopped
- 1 egg
- 1 tbsp oregano, dry
- 1 tsp chili powder
- ½ tsp cumin

For the Soup:

- 4 carrots, chopped
- 3 cloves garlic, chopped
- ½ onion, chopped
- 2 tbsp olive oil
- 1 can, 14.5 oz. roasted diced tomatoes
- 2 x 32 oz organic chicken broth
- 1 tsp salt

- Pepper

- 2/3 cup white rice, uncooked

- Cilantro, fresh

Directions:

1. To make your meatballs, mix all ingredients together in a mixing bowl and blend well. Form meatballs into 1 ½ inch diameters. You will get 16 to 18 meatballs.

2. Place meatballs in the fridge to set.

3. To make the soup, set your Instant Pot to sauté and add the oil. Sauté the onions and garlic with fragrant and translucent. Next, toss in the carrots and tomatoes and cook till carrots are just about tender.

4. Turn sauté function off, and then pour in the broth and rice. Place meatballs gently on top the rice gently, one at a time.

5. Lock and close the Instant Pot then press Manual and cook on high pressure for 10 minutes.

6. When cooking is done, release pressure manually then switch pot off.

7. Stir soup and taste test with salt and pepper.

8. Serve soup hot and garnish with parsley.

Instant Pot Cod Chowder

Total Preparation & Cook Time: 35 minutes

Servings – 6

Nutritional info: Calories: 1956, Fats: 75.6g, Carbs: 153g, Protein: 174.9g, Fiber: 15.9g, Sugar: 21g

Ingredients:

- 2 tbsp butter
- 1 cup onion, chopped
- ½ mushrooms, sliced
- 4 cups potatoes, peeled & diced
- 4 cups organic chicken broth
- 2 lb cod
- 1 tsp old bay seasoning
- 1 cup clam juice
- ½ cup flour
- 1 can evaporated milk
- Salt & pepper to taste
- Garnish: 4-6 slices bacon

Directions:

1. In your Instant Pot, pour 1 cup of water and place a trivet inside.

2. To this, lay a few pieces of your cod on the trivet close and lock the lid and press Manual to cook on high for 9 minutes. Release pressure manually.

3. Remove the cod and dice it into chunks.

4. Remove trivet and throw away water from the pot. Clean pot and then press Sauté.

5. When the pot heats up, add in the butter and sauté onions and mushrooms till they are soft.

6. Toss in the potatoes and cook another 5 minutes then add the chicken broth.

7. Close and lock the lid, then close the valve too. Press Manual and cook on high pressure for 8 minutes.

8. When the cooking is done, release the pot's pressure and then season with Old Bay, salt, and pepper. Pour in the clam juice followed by the flour and blend well. Stir in the fish chunks.

9. Pour in the condensed milk and blend well again.

10. Serve soup hot with buttered bread rolls.

Instant Pot Creamy Celery Soup

Total Preparation & Cook Time: 20 minutes

Servings – 6

Nutritional info: Calories: 1456, Fats: 114g, Carbs: 153g, Protein: 21g, Fiber: 12g, Sugar: 9.6g

Ingredients

- 1 head of celery
- 1 large potato, peeled and chopped
- 1 medium onion, quartered
- ½ cup butter, unsalted
- 3 cups organic low-sodium chicken broth
- ¼ cup fresh dill
- ½ cup heavy cream
- ½ tsp coriander
- 1 tsp salt

Directions:

1. Into your Instant pot, toss in the celery, potato, onions and butter.

2. Pour in your broth and put the lid on. Click on Manual and cook on high pressure for 10 minutes.

3. When the cooking has completed, perform quick release and check vegetables to see if it's tender.

4. Then using an immersion blender, puree the contents. Add in dill and puree again.

5. Add in your heavy cream and season with salt and pepper and sprinkle with coriander.

6. To serve, pour soup into bowls and garnish with celery leaves.

Light and Easy Broccoli Soup in the Instant Pot

Total Preparation & Cook Time: 10 minutes

Servings – 6

Nutritional info: Calories: 1139, Fats: 98g, Carbs: 27g, Protein: 21g, Fiber: 4.2g, Sugar: 11g

Ingredients:

- 1 tbsp organic coconut oil
- 1 head of broccoli
- 2-3 carrots diced
- ½ onion, diced
- 1-2 cloves garlic, minced
- 4-6 cups low sodium chicken broth
- 8 lb cream cheese
- Garnish: sliced green onions & shredded cheese
- Salt & pepper to taste

Directions:

1. Turn on your Instant Pot and click sauté. Pour the coconut oil in and sauté the garlic and onions.

2. Shut down the pot and throw in your broccoli, carrots, and chicken broth. Stir once, put a lid on and then press SOUP to cook for 5 minutes. Walk away.

3. When cooking is done, perform a quick release.

4. Use an immersion blender to blend soup to desired consistency, inside the pot.

5. To this, add in the cream cheese and season with salt and pepper.

6. Once the cheese has melted, stir everything together once more.

7. To serve, place in bowls and garnish with green onions and cheese.

Chapter 7- Seafood

Instant Pot Seafood Paella

Total Preparation & Cook Time: 1 hours

Servings – 4

Nutritional info: Calories: 1471, Fats: 3,1g, Carbs: 324g, Protein: 30g, Fiber: 10g, Sugar: 17g

Ingredients:
Fish Stock:

- 4 cod fish head
- 2 carrots
- 1 celery
- 1 bay leaf
- Bunch of parsley with stems
- 6 cups of water

Paella:

- 2 cups short-grain rice
- 4 tbsp EVOO
- 1 medium Yellow onion diced
- 1 red bell pepper - diced
- 1 green bell pepper - diced
- Saffron powder
- 1 ¾ cups low sodium vegetable stock

- ⅛ tsp ground turmeric

- 2 tsp sea salt

- 1 cup of seafood

- 2 cups of mixed shellfish

Directions:

1. For the fish stock, add in all ingredients into the Instant Pot and cook on high pressure for 5 minutes. When the timer goes off, naturally release pressure. Set aside.

2. For the Paella, set the Instant Pot to Sauté and heat EVOO. Once the oil gets hot, toss in onions and add peppers. Sauté till onions are soft and tender.

3. Add in the saffron, seafood, and rice. Sauté everything for 2 minutes.

4. Pour in the fish stock and add salt and turmeric. Mix well.

5. Arrange shellfish on top but do not to mix.

6. Close the pot and lock the lid and set to cook on high pressure for 6 minutes

7. Use natural pressure to release steam once cooker timer goes off. Once all pressure and steam are gone, open the lid and mix paella well. Let sit for 1 minute before serving. Garnish with chopped cilantro.

Sweet & Spicy Mahi Mahi Instant Pot

Total Preparation & Cook Time: 35 hours

Servings – 4

Nutritional info: Calories: 162, Fats: 0g, Carbs: 44.5g, Protein: 0.3g, Fiber: 10g, Sugar: 35g

Ingredients:

- 2 mahi-mahi fillets
- Salt, to taste
- Cracked black pepper, to taste
- 1-2 cloves garlic, minced or crushed
- 1" piece ginger, finely grated
- ½ lime, juiced
- 2 tbsp honey
- 1 tbsp Nanami Togarashi
- 2 tbsp hot sauce
- 1 tbsp orange juice

Directions:

1. Season mahi-mahi with salt and pepper. Set aside.

2. In a bowl, combine ginger, garlic, honey and lime juice together with Sriracha, Nanami Togarashi and orange juice to make the sweet and spicy sauce.

3. In the Instant pot, add in one cup of water.

4. Insert the steam rack to the bottom of the pot. Place the salmon fillets on the rack in one layer.

5. Pour the sauce over the fillets. Cover and lock the lid.

6. Press Manual and adjust cook time to 5 minutes.

7. Once done, the beeper goes off and switch the valve from sealing to venting to allow pressure to release.

8. Once all pressure is gone, open the lid.

9. Serve Mahi-Mahi warm with a side of salad.

Wild Alaskan Cod

Total Preparation & Cook Time: 30 minutes

Servings – 4

Nutritional info: Calories: 263, Fats: 23.4g, Carbs: 7.05g, Protein: 1.8g, Fiber: 2.2g, Sugar: 4.8g

Ingredients:

- 1 large fillet of cod

- 1 cup of cherry tomatoes

- Salt and pepper for seasoning

- 2 tbsp butter

Directions:

1. Using an oven safe glass dish that fits your Instant Pot, place the tomatoes inside

2. Cut the cod filler into 2 to 3 smaller pieces and lay it on top of the tomatoes.

3. Season with salt and pepper and top it with butter.

4. Drizzle the olive oil.

5. In the Instant Pot, pour in one cup water and place a trivet inside and set the glass dish on it.

6. Lock the lid and press Manual and cook for 5 minutes on high pressure.

7. Once beeper goes off, release pressure manually.

8. Serve cod with warm salad

Spicy Lemon Salmon

Total Preparation & Cook Time: 30 minutes

Servings – 4

Nutritional info: Calories: 40, Fats: 5.4g, Carbs: 3.05g, Protein: 21.8g, Fiber: 2.2g, Sugar: 0.8g

Ingredients:

- 3 large salmon fillets
- 2 lemons, 1 juiced and 1 sliced
- 1-2 tbsp Nanami Togarashi
- Sea salt and pepper to taste
- 1 cup water

Directions:

1. Season salmon generously with lemon juice, Nanami, pepper and salt
2. Insert steel rack inside bottom of Instant Pot. Keep handles up.
3. Add one cup of water to pot.
4. Next, place seasoned salmon on steam rack in a single layer.
5. Pour leftover lemon juice and seasoning on the fillets
6. Cover and lock the Instant Pot lid.
7. Select Manual and adjust the timer to 5 minutes. Make sure Valve is at Seal and not at Vent.
8. When the pot beeps, your salmon has finished cooking. Manually release pressure to avoid remaining steam from over cooking the salmon.
9. Serve Salmon with a side of salad.

Steamed Asparagus and Shrimp

Total Preparation & Cook Time: 15 minutes

Servings – 4

Nutritional info: Calories: 40, Fats: 4.7g, Carbs: 0.05g, Protein: 0.18g, Fiber: 0.2g, Sugar: 0.g

Ingredients:

- 1 lb peeled and deveined shrimp
- 1 bunch of asparaguses
- 1 tsp olive oil
- ½ tbsp Cajun seasoning

Directions:

1. To the Instant Pot, add in 1 cup of water
2. Insert steam racks to the bottom of the Instant Pot with handles facing up.
3. Place asparagus on the steam rack in a single layer. This acts as a bed for the shrimp.
4. Next, arrange shrimp on the asparagus.
5. Season the shrimp with olive oil and Cajun seasoning.
6. Cover and lock the lid.
7. Press Steam and adjust for 2 minutes cook time on Low Pressure. Switch the valve to sealing.
8. Once the pot beeps, manually release the pressure and turn valve to venting.
9. To serve, place asparagus and shrimp, drizzle some olive oil and some Parmesan cheese.

Instant Pot Shrimp Fried Rice

Total Preparation & Cook Time: 35 minutes

Servings – 6

Nutritional info: Calories: 606, Fats: 51.2g, Carbs: 21g, Protein: 19.4g, Fiber: 31.5g, Sugar: 6.9g

Ingredients:

- 2 cups brown rice
- 2 large eggs, beaten
- 3 tbsp sesame seed oil
- 1 cup chopped onions
- ¼ cup soy sauce
- 4 cloves garlic
- 12 oz bag frozen shrimp peeled and tailed
- 1 ½ cups frozen peas and carrots
- 4 cups water
- ¼ tsp cayenne pepper
- Salt and pepper to taste
- ½ tsp ground ginger

Directions:

1. Wash and rinse the rice till the water is clear.
2. On the Instant Pot, click Sauté and allow pot to heat up.
3. Next, pour in 2 tbsp of the sesame oil and scramble eggs when the oil starts to bubble

4. Once done, remove eggs and set aside

5. Heat up the remaining oil and toss in minced garlic and chopped onions. Sauté till translucent

6. Turn off Sauté and then add in peas, carrots and shrimps

7. Pour in washed rice into pot then add in soy sauce, ginger, salt and pepper.

8. Pour water in and give everything a healthy mixture

9. Cover the Instant pot and click on rice.

10. Set valve to pressure and allow cooking. Walk away.

11. When timer goes off, give the rice another stir and leave for another 5 minutes.

12. Serve rice warm with sliced scallions or fried omelets.

Instant Pot Drunken Clams

Total Preparation & Cook Time: 15 minutes

Servings – 6

Nutritional info: Calories: 1711, Fats: 51g, Carbs: 153g, Protein: 11.4g, Fiber: 6.5g, Sugar: 46.9g

Ingredients:

- ¼ cup extra virgin olive oil
- 2 cloves garlic, peeled and minced
- ¼ cup finely chopped fresh basil
- 2 cups pale ale
- 1 cup water
- ½ cup chicken broth
- ¼ cup dry white wine
- 3 lb fresh clams, clean
- 2 tbsp freshly squeezed lemon juice

Directions:

- Click on Sauté and heat olive oil in Instant Pot. Once Pot is slightly hot, add in minced garlic and cook until fragrant. Stir in chopped basil and add in chicken broth, wine, lemon juice and water.
- Allow mixture to come to a boil, cook for 1 minute
- With the mixture still inside, place a trivet into the pot and place steamer basket. Place cleaned clams into the basket.

- Close and lock pot and set Manual to cook on high pressure for 5 minutes.

- Once beeper goes off, switch pot off and do a quick release. Check clams and discard any that aren't open.

- Remove basket from pot and transfer cooked clams to serving bowl. Pour liquid into pot over clams and serve immediately.

Tiger Prawn Seafood Risotto

Total Preparation & Cook Time: 45 minutes

Servings – 4

Nutritional info: Calories: 2211, Fats: 94g, Carbs: 221g, Protein: 33.4g, Fiber: 10g, Sugar: 0g

Ingredients:

- 3 tbsp olive oil

- 4 tbsp unsalted butter

- 3 medium cloves garlic, minced

- 1 medium shallot, minced

- 2 cups Arborio rice

- ¾ cup cooking sake

- 4 cups homemade fish stock

- 2 tsp Japanese soy sauce

- 2.5 tbsp white miso paste

- ½ tsp salt

- ½ lb tiger prawns, frozen, unpeeled

- ⅛ tsp baking soda

- 1 ½ tbsp Parmesan cheese, finely grated

- 1 cup Parmesan cheese grated

- 2 stalks spring onions, thinly sliced

Directions:

1. Press Sauté on your Instant Pot and allow the pot to heat up. Press Adjust once to increase heat. Your Pot should indicate HOT.

2. When it shows HOT, pour in the olive oil and butter, coat bottom of the pot. Sauté the shallots, minced garlic till fragrant. Then add in tiger prawns and cook till prawns are about 80% done. Remove and set aside.

3. Into the garlic butter oil, pour in the rice and stir to evenly coat with the oil. After two to three minutes, the edges of the rice should become translucent. Now, pour in the Japanese soy sauce and your miso paste and mix well with rice.

4. Pour in your cooking sake, and then deglaze the pot. Allow the sake to boil for a minute to allow the alcohol to evaporate.

5. Next, pour in the fish stock and clean the sides of the pot to make sure no rice or shallot sticks to it. Close and lock the lid of your Instant Pot and set to cook on High pressure for 5 minutes.

6. While your risotto is cooking, peel your prawns.

7. Then perform the quick release. If you prefer a softer risotto, then add one more minute of cook time.

8. Next, use a spatula to stir your risotto to form a smooth and creamy mixture. If the risotto is too runny, then allow cooking for another minute.

9. Toss in the parmesan cheese and the green onions. Stir to combine. Season and taste.

10. To serve, place risotto and arrange prawns on top. Serve with more parmesan cheese while warm.

Instant Pot Jambalaya

Total Preparation & Cook Time: 20 minutes

Servings – 6

Nutritional info: Calories: 3618, Fats: 163g, Carbs: 300g, Protein: 211.4g, Fiber: 17g, Sugar: 33g

Ingredients:

- 2 tbsp olive oil
- 1 lb Andouille sausage, pre-cooked & sliced
- 1 lb chicken breasts & thighs, diced
- 1 lb prawns
- 2 cups multi-color bell peppers, diced
- 2 cups yellow onions, finely diced
- 2 tbsp garlic, minced
- 1 ½ cups rice
- 3 ½ cups chicken stock
- 1 cup crushed tomatoes
- 1 tbsp + 1 tsp Creole seasoning
- 1 tbsp Worcestershire sauce

Directions:

1. Press Sauté on your Instant Pot

2. While pot is heating up, in a separate dish coat chicken with Creole seasoning. Place chicken in pot and brown on all sides.

3. Once done, take out and set chicken aside.

4. To the similar pot, add in peppers, onions and garlic. Sauté till onions are translucent

5. Next, add in rice and stir to coat mixture.

6. Combine tomato puree, remaining Creole seasoning, Worcestershire and the chicken

7. Close and lock lid then click on rice.

8. Allow pot to cook and walk away.

9. Once rice is cooked, add in the prawns and sausage.

10. Place lid back on and press 'Manual' and allow cooking for another 2 minutes.

11. Serve jambalaya warm.

Instant Pot Orange Ginger Fish

Total Preparation & Cook Time: 20 minutes

Servings – 4

Nutritional info: Calories: 3618, Fats: 163g, Carbs: 300g, Protein: 211.4g, Fiber: 17g, Sugar: 33g

Ingredients:

- 4 white fish fillets
- Juice and zest from 1 orange
- 1 cup fish stock or white wine
- 3 to 4 spring onions
- Thumb size piece of ginger, chopped
- Olive oil
- Salt and pepper

Directions:

1. Dry your fish fillets with a paper towel. Pour some olive oil and rub the fillets. Season lightly with salt and pepper.

2. Into your Instant Pot, pour the fish stock or white wine then add the ginger, spring onions, orange juice and zest.

3. Place a steamer basket into the pressure cooker and place your fish inside this.

4. Close and lock the lid of your cooker and cook on high for 7 minutes.

5. Once timer goes off, perform quick release then remove fish from basket.

6. To serve, place fish on serving dish with a side of fresh salad. Generously pour the sauce from the pot over the fish.

Chapter 8- Snacks

Dulce de Leche in the Instant Pot

Total Preparation & Cook Time: 15 minutes

Servings – 6

Nutritional info: Calories: 355, Fats: 78g, Carbs: 0.02g, Protein: 0. g, Fiber: 0g, Sugar: 165.g

Ingredients:

- 1 can sweetened condensed milk
- 2 canning jars with lid and ring
- Water

Directions:

1. Using the two 8 oz canning jars, divide the sweetened condensed milk equally. Close jars tightly with lid and rings.

2. Place steam rack in the bottom of Instant Pot and place jars on the rack.

3. Pour enough water into the Instant Pot so that it reaches half way up the side of the jars.

4. Cover and lock the Pot lid.

5. Press Manual and adjust cooking time to 30 minutes. Switch valve to Sealing.

6. Once timer beeps, turn off the Pot and allow pressure to release naturally.

7. With oven mitts, remove jars from the Instant Pot and let it cool completely for 15 minutes before you open.

8. Open the can and stir thoroughly to smooth out the dulce de leche.

Instant Pot Applesauce

Total Preparation & Cook Time: 45 minutes

Servings – 4

Nutritional info: Calories: 1409, Fats: 4.7g, Carbs: 357g, Protein: 7.5g, Fiber: 68.4g, Sugar: 278g

Ingredients:

- 12 organic apples, peeled and quartered
- ½ lemon juice
- 2 tbsp unsalted butter
- 1 tbsp ground cinnamon
- 1 tbsp raw honey
- ¼ tsp sea salt
- 1 cup filtered water

Directions:

1. Wash, prep and quarter all your apples and place them in a stainless steel bowl.

2. Mix butter, cinnamon, honey and sea salt together with the apples.

3. Place the bowl inside the Instant pot, secure and lock the lid.

4. Make sure vent is in sealed and turn on your Instant Pot.

5. Press the Manual button and cook on high pressure for 3 minutes.

6. Walk away and let the cooker cook.

7. When done cooking, the Pot will beep and press 'Keep Warm/Cancel' button and then turn off the Instant Pot.

8. Leave pot for 15 minutes while pressure is released naturally.

9. Once this is done, remove the lid and ladle apples into high pressured blender or food processor.

10. Pulse until apples are fully combined and smooth, to desired consistency. Add leftover liquid if too thick.

11. Enjoy applesauce warm or cold.

Creamy Rice Pudding

Total Preparation & Cook Time: 30 Minutes

Servings – 6

Nutritional info: Calories: 120, Fats: 2.1g, Carbs: 27g, Protein: 4.2g, Fiber: 0.2g, Sugar: 0.1g

Ingredients:

- 2 cups full cream milk
- 1 ¼ cup water
- ¾ cup coconut cream
- 1 cup basmati rice
- 1 tsp vanilla extract
- ¼ cup maple syrup
- ½ tsp salt

Directions:

1. Using a fine mesh colander, place the rice into it and rinse it a few times till the water turns clear
2. Place rice in the Instant Pot and add milk, water, maple syrup and salt
3. Stir briefly to combine ingredients.
4. Close vent and seal the lid
5. Press Porridge button for 20 minutes cook time.
6. When timer goes off, release pressure slowly for 10 minutes
7. After 10 minutes, press Cancel and open vent followed by the lid
8. Add in cream and vanilla and stir well to combine.
9. Serve with optional toppings such as fresh fruit, jam, nuts and butter.

Instant Pot Candied Orange

Total Preparation & Cook Time: 50 Minutes

Servings – 10

Nutritional info: Calories: 1275, Fats: 46.2g, Carbs: 10g, Protein: 151g, Fiber: 1.3g, Sugar: 2.9g

Ingredients:

- 3 medium oranges
- 2 cups sugar
- 5 cups water

Directions:

1. Cut orange peel into ¼ inch wide strips.

2. Placed strips into your Instant Pot and add four cups of water. Cook on high pressure for 3 minutes.

3. When cooking is done, release pressure slowly. Discard water.

4. Into the pot on Sauté, add 2 cups of sugar and 1 cup water and cook on medium heat. Stir mixture occasionally until sugar has dissolved.

5. Close and lock lid. Cook for another 10 minutes on high pressure

6. Meanwhile, strain the peels and cool them on a cookie sheet.

7. Once the sugar has dissolved, turn Instant Pot off and allow mixture to slightly cool but not harden.

8. Pour sugar into a bowl and place peels a few at a time to coat.

9. When evenly coated, place peels on a newly lined cookie sheet and let them dry overnight in the fridge.

Instant Pot Stuffed Peaches

Total Preparation & Cook Time: 15 Minutes

Servings – 10

Nutritional info: Calories: 775, Fats: 36.2g, Carbs: 33.7g, Protein: 231.7g, Fiber: 66.9g, Sugar: 66.9g

Ingredients:

- 5 medium organic peaches
- 1/4 cup cassava flour
- 1/4 cup maple sugar
- 1/2 tsp ground cinnamon
- 1/4 tsp pure almond extract
- 2 tbsp butter
- Pinch pink sea salt

Directions:

1. Prepare the peaches by slicing off ¼ of the top of the fruits. Remove pits and hollow out the middle but keeping the peaches intact. Use a paring knife or spoon. Set aside.

2. In a mixing bowl, prepare the crumble mixture by combining cassava flour, sweetener, cinnamon, butter, almond extract and salt. Mix everything together with clean hands until mixture is crumbly.

3. Fill each peach with the crumble mixture.

4. Next, place a steamer basket inside the instant pot and pour in water and ¼ tsp of the almond extract.

5. Carefully place stuffed peaches inside the steamer basket.

6. Close and lock the lid then set the valve to seal.

7. Press Manual and decrease cook time to 3 minutes.

8. Once the pot beeps, press 'Keep Warm/Cancel' and unplug your Pot. Perform a quick release to open the steam release valve.

9. Open the lid when the silver dial drops, and the steam venting stops.

10. Carefully lift the steamer basket and place it on a dish to rest and cool

11. To serve, arrange peaches on serving plate and serve with a scoop of vanilla ice cream.

Instant Pot Popcorn

Total Preparation & Cook Time: 10 Minutes

Servings – 10

Nutritional info: Calories: 555, Fats: 63g, Carbs: 0.7g, Protein: 0.2g, Fiber: 0g, Sugar: 0g

Ingredients:

- 3 tbsp coconut oil

- 2 tbsp butter

- ½ cup popcorn kernels

Directions:

1. Click Sauté on your pot and then press on Adjust '+' to increase the cooking time

2. When the Pot reads HOT, pour in the coconut oil and butter and allow to melt and combine

3. Toss in the kernels and stir it around to make sure the butter and oil covers all the kernels.

4. Add more oil if necessary.

5. Close and lock lid and let kernels pop inside

6. When a half of the corn has popped, turn your pot off and allow the rest to pop from the remaining heat.

7. Sprinkle salt and other additional seasoning of choice.

8. Serve warm.

Instant Pot Candied Lemon Peel

Total Preparation & Cook Time: 20 minutes

Servings – 10

Nutritional info: Calories: 1265, Fats: 45g, Carbs: 15g, Protein: 511, Fiber: 2g, Sugar: 3.1g

Ingredients:

- 5 medium lemons
- 2 cups sugar
- 5 cups water

Directions:

1. Cut orange peel into ¼ inch wide strips.

2. Placed strips into your Instant Pot and add four cups of water. Cook on high pressure for 3 minutes.

3. When cooking is done, release pressure slowly. Discard water.

4. Into the pot on Sauté, add 2 cups of sugar and 1 cup water and cook on medium heat. Stir mixture occasionally until sugar has dissolved.

5. Close and lock lid. Cook on high pressure for another 10 minutes.

6. Meanwhile, strain the peels and cool them on a cookie sheet.

7. Once sugar has dissolved, turn Instant Pot off and allow mixture to slightly cool but not harden.

8. Pour sugar into a bowl and place peels a few at a time to coat.

9. When evenly coated, place peels on a newly lined cookie sheet and let them dry overnight in the fridge.

Pressure Cooker Corn on the Cob

Total Preparation & Cook Time: 20 minutes

Servings – 10

Nutritional info: Calories: 1265, Fats: 45g, Carbs: 15g, Protein: 511, Fiber: 2g, Sugar: 3.1g

Ingredients:

2 cups water

Fresh ears of corn

Directions:

1. Into the Instant Pot, pour in 2 cups of water. Place a steamer basket and the corn into the basket.

2. Lock and close the lid. Select High Pressure and cook for two or three minutes.

3. When the beeper goes off, turn off the Instant Pot and perform a quick pressure release.

4. Once the valve drops, remove the lid to release remaining pressure.

5. Remove the corn from the cob and sprinkle with salt and brush with butter.

Pressure Cooker Southern Peanuts

Total Preparation & Cook Time: 1 hour

Servings – 10

Nutritional info: Calories: 3365, Fats: 15g, Carbs: 65g, Protein: 331g, Fiber: 42g, Sugar: 2.1g

Ingredients:

- 1 lb raw peanuts
- ½ tsp sea salt
- Water
- Garnish: sugar

Directions:

1. Rinse and remove any twigs from the peanuts.
2. Toss in peanuts into the Instant pot and cover with enough water but to not fully soak. Cover peanuts with trivet.
3. Close and lock lid and close pressure valve.
4. Cook on high pressure for 40 minutes.
5. Allow pressure to release naturally when cooking is done. If peanuts are too hard, allow peanuts to sit in Pot for another 10 minutes.
6. Season peanuts with sugar.

Instant Pot Candied Pecans

Total Preparation & Cook Time: 1 hour

Servings – 10

Nutritional info: Calories: 1092, Fats: 0.2g, Carbs: 242g, Protein: 0.5g, Fiber: 5g, Sugar: 217g

Ingredients:

- 1 egg white
- 1 cup sugar
- ½ cup brown sugar
- 1.5 tbsp cinnamon
- 2 tsp vanilla
- 4 cups pecans
- ¼ cup water

Directions:

1. In a mixing bowl, blend the white sugar, brown sugar, and cinnamon. Stir and set aside.

2. In another mixing bowl, combine the egg whites and vanilla. Whisk together until mixture becomes frothy.

3. In your instant pot, toss pecans in and pour in the egg white mixture. Stir pecans with the mixture to coat evenly.

4. After this, sprinkle over your cinnamon sugar over the pecans and make sure to cover all sides.

5. Turn on your pot and click Manual. Cook on high pressure for 20 minutes, stirring occasionally.

6. Once your 20 minutes are over, pour in the water and stir again. The water ill makes the shells crunchy.

7. Close pot and cook for another 10 minutes.

8. When cooking time is off, perform a quick pressure release.

9. Remove pecans from the pot and spread over a cookie sheet. Leave to cool before eating.

10. Store in air tight container which can last for three weeks.

Corn and Jalapeno Dip in an Instant Pot

Total Preparation & Cook Time: 45minutes

Servings – 8

Nutritional info: Calories: 1762, Fats: 70.2g, Carbs: 992g, Protein: 21g, Fiber: 33g, Sugar: 17g

Ingredients:

- 8 oz cream cheese, cubed
- 4 slices bacon diced
- 3 cans whole kernel corn drained
- ½ cup sour cream
- 1 cup shredded pepper Jack cheese
- ¼ cup grated Parmesan cheese
- Salt and ground black pepper, to taste
- 2 jalapenos seeded and diced
- 2 tbsp chopped chives

Directions:

1. Turn on your Instant Pot and click on Sauté. When the pot gets hot, add in the diced bacon and cook until it turns crispy and brown Transfer cooked bacon to a place and set aside.

2. Clean pot and toss in corn, jalapenos, sour cream, and cheeses. Season mixture with salt and pepper. Stir mixture till everything looks well combined. Carefully place cream cheese in one layer, covering the surface of the mixture.

3. Close and lock the lid and click Manual. Cook on high pressure for 30 minutes.

4. When pot starts to beep, perform natural pressure release.

5. When done, open pot and stir contents till everything are well combined.

6. To serve, garnish with bacon and chives.

Instant Pot S'mores Brownies

Total Preparation & Cook Time: 45minutes

Servings – 15

Nutritional info: Calories: 2310, Fats: 116.2g, Carbs: 732g, Protein: 10g, Fiber: 23g, Sugar: 220g

Ingredients:

For the Crust:

- 3 cups graham cracker crumbs
- ¾ cup butter, melted
- ½ cup sugar

For the Brownies:

- ½ cup butter
- 1 cup sugar
- 3 large eggs
- 1 ¼ cups all-purpose flour
- 8 oz bittersweet chocolate, chopped
- ¼ cup unsweetened cocoa powder
- 1 cup semisweet chocolate chips
- ¾ tsp baking powder
- ½ tsp salt

Topping:

- 4 Hershey milk chocolate bars
- 10 oz mini marshmallows

Directions:

1. Prepare your 7-inch springform by lining it with a sheet of parchment paper. Grease it with butter or non-stick cooking spray.

2. To make the crust, mix the crumbs together with melted butter and the sugar. Press mixture into the bottom of your springform pan and use offset spatula to form an even layer.

3. To make the brownies, mix chocolate together with butter and microwave till it melts.

4. Remove from heat and slowly mix in the sugar. When evenly combined, mix the eggs one at a time, mixing after each egg drop.

5. In another mixing bowl, blend cocoa powder, flour, baking powder, and salt. Add in the chocolate chips.

6. Blend the wet ingredients together with the dry ingredients. Evenly spread the batter into the prepared pan, over the crust.

7. Chop the Hershey's bar into chunks and place them in one layer on the dough.

8. Place trivet into pot and pour in 2 cups water.

9. Cover pan with foil and place on top of the trivet. Close valve and lock the lid.

10. Click Manual and cook on high pressure for 30 minutes.

11. Once brownies have completed cooking, perform quick pressure release and open top. Place marshmallows on top and press 'Warm/Cancel' button for 5 minutes or till marshmallows have softened.

12. To serve, remove brownies from pan and allow to cool. Once cooled, cut into pieces and serve with vanilla ice cream.

Chapter 9- Recipe for Kids

Sweet & Sour Chicken

Total Preparation & Cook Time: 30 minutes

Servings – 6

Nutritional info: Calories: 1079, Fats: 17g, Carbs: 261g, Protein: 132g, Fiber: 0g, Sugar: 228g

Ingredients:

- 1 lb diced chicken breast
- ¼ cup cornstarch
- 1 cup sugar
- 1 can dice pineapples
- ½ cup vinegar
- ½ cup water
- ½ cup ketchup
- 1 tbsp soy sauce
- 1 green or red bell pepper
- Rice of choice
- Sesame seeds for garnish

Directions:

1. In your Instant Pot, click Sauté and combine sugar, water, vinegar, pineapple, ketchup, diced bell pepper and soy sauce. Stir all ingredients until sugar has dissolved.

2. Toss chicken in and click on Manual and cook on High Pressure for 20 minutes.

3. Once the beeper goes off, naturally release steam. Once done, remove from Pot and serve with steamed rice.

Sweet Pork

Total Preparation & Cook Time: 55 minutes

Servings – 4

Nutritional info: Calories: 551, Fats: 0.7g, Carbs: 142g, Protein: 0.5g, Fiber: 0g, Sugar: 140.g

Ingredients:

- 1 lb pork butt roast
- 1 packet of taco seasonings
- 1 can soda (Coca Cola)
- 1 cup brown sugar

Directions:

1. Mix all dry ingredients together and dry rub on pork.
2. Turn on Instant Pot and click on 'Meat/Stew'.
3. Place pork inside pot and pour Coca-Cola until it covers nearly the top of the pork, but not submerged.
4. Close and lock lid. Make sure vent is sealed.
5. Let Pot cook and walk away.
6. Once beeper goes off, allow for natural steam release and then switch valve to vent.
7. Remove pork from pot, shred into pieces and serve with steamed vegetables and potato mash.

Chicken & Rice Soup

Total Preparation & Cook Time: 50 minutes

Servings – 4

Nutritional info: Calories: 2255, Fats: 110.2g, Carbs: 227g, Protein: 56.3g, Fiber: 11.8g, Sugar: 37.5g

Ingredients:

- 4 boneless, skinless chicken breasts
- 8 cups low sodium chicken broth
- 2 tbsp chicken seasoning
- 1 cup uncooked rice
- 1 medium onion diced fine
- 1 cup carrots, chopped

- 1 cup celery, chopped
- 1 tbsp garlic, minced
- 1 cup water
- 1 stick butter
- ½ cup wheat flour
- 2 cups milk
- 2 bay leaves
- Salt and pepper to taste

Directions:

1. Wash and rinse rice with water. In your Instant Pot, layer with uncooked rice then uncooked chicken breast and toss in onions, garlic, carrots, bay leaves, water, chicken broth and seasoning.

2. Turn pot on and click 'Soup.' Cover and lock the lid and make sure Valve is set to seal.

3. Cook on high pressure for 10 minutes.

4. When beeper goes off, remove chicken from the instant

185

pot and let cool. Then shred with forks. Allow the rice to keep cooking in the remaining steam.

5. Place the chicken back in when the rice has cooked.

6. In a small saucepan, melt butter and toss in the flour. Let the mixture cook for 1 minute then whisk in milk slowly. Whisk until all lumps are gone. Let the mixture thicken and become creamy.

7. Add the cream mixture to the Instant Pot. Stir well to combine.

8. If the soup is too thick, add some water.

9. Season with salt and pepper and serve hot with bread rolls.

Spiced Apple Baked Beans

Total Preparation & Cook Time: 15 minutes

Servings – 6

Nutritional info: Calories: 2220, Fats: 189g, Carbs: 28.3g, Protein: 170g, Fiber: 5.1g, Sugar: 9.8g

Ingredients:

- 3 cups onions, minced
- 3 cans baked beans
- 1 can apple pie filling
- 1 lb bacon, cooked and crumbled
- 2 cloves, 1 stick cinnamon, salt, and pepper to taste

Directions:

1. Turn on the Instant Pot and click to Manual.
2. Add all ingredients into the Instant Pot and cook on high pressure for 15 minutes, stirring occasionally.
3. Once onions are soft and translucent and when the timer beeps, it's time to eat!
4. Serve while hot with toasted baguette.

Honey Barbeque Chicken Sandwich

Total Preparation & Cook Time: 45 minutes

Servings – 4

Nutritional info: Calories: 551, Fats: 33g, Carbs: 53g, Protein: 0.13g, Fiber: 0g, Sugar: 51g

Ingredients:

- 3 boneless skinless chicken breasts
- 1 bottle honey BBQ sauce
- 2 tbsp Worcestershire sauce
- ½ cup Italian salad dressing
- ¼ cup brown sugar

Directions:

1. In a bowl, blend barbecue with the Worcestershire sauce, salad dressing and sugar
2. Place chicken in Instant Pot and transfer sauce over chicken, spreading evenly
3. Close and lock lid and cook on high pressure for 30 minutes.
4. When timer goes off, allow pressure to release naturally
5. Take chicken out from Pot and use forks to shred
6. Transfer the shredded chicken back into pot and mix to coat with sauce.
7. Serve warm with Kaiser rolls

Grape Jelly BBQ Meatballs

Total Preparation & Cook Time: 25 minutes

Servings – 8

Nutritional info: Calories: 355, Fats: 44.7g, Carbs: 16.02g, Protein: 4.13g, Fiber: 0g, Sugar: 7.1g

Ingredients:

- 1 bag frozen meatballs (about 50 pieces)
- 1 bottle BBQ sauce
- 1 jar grape jelly

Directions:

1. Combine well in a bowl, the BBQ sauce, and grape jelly.
2. Coat the meatballs in the sauce.
3. Place the meatballs into the Instant Pot and cook on high pressure for 15 minutes.
4. Serve over pasta or enjoy as appetizer.

Instant Pot Tater Tot Casserole

Total Preparation & Cook Time: 45 minutes

Servings – 4

Nutritional info: Calories: 2056, Fats: 120g, Carbs: 31g, Protein: 210g, Fiber: 1.7g, Sugar: 5.8g

Ingredients:

- 16 oz package of tater tots
- 1 lb ground beef, browned
- 1 can Rotel tomatoes
- 2 cups cheddar cheese, shredded
- 1 can cream of chicken soup
- 1 small onion

Directions:

1. Turn on Instant Pot and click on sauté. Brown beef, onions, and Rotel. Stir well to combine.

2. Once done, mix in cream of chicken soup and top the mixture with tater tots, spreading evenly.

3. Turn on 'Meat/Stew' and adjust the time to cook for 30 minutes on High pressure.

4. Once beeper starts beeping, cooking is done. Allow pressure to release naturally.

5. To serve, sprinkle cheese on top.

Slow Cooker Chili

Total Preparation & Cook Time: 45 minutes

Servings – 6

Nutritional info: Calories: 2051, Fats: 64g, Carbs: 161g, Protein: 317g, Fiber: 0g, Sugar: 100g

Ingredients:

- 2 lb lean ground organic beef
- 2 med onions, chopped
- 2 cups chopped bell peppers
- 2 tbsp chili powder
- 1 can dice tomatoes
- 1 can crush tomatoes
- 1 can low sodium tomato paste
- 1 can black beans, drained and rinsed
- 1 can low sodium beef broth
- 1 tsp hot sauce
- 2 tsp sugar
- 2 cans kidney beans drained and rinsed
- 1 tbsp Worcestershire sauce
- 1 tsp dried basil
- 1 tbsp dried oregano
- 1 tsp freshly ground black pepper
- 3 cloves garlic, minced

Directions:

1. In the Instant Pot, click on Sauté and brown the beef, 5 minutes.

2. Drain the fat off the pot. Next, add onions, peppers, and garlic.
   Cook till veggies are tender.

3. Next, click on the Manual button to cook, close and lock lid and allow cooking for 30 minutes. Ensure the pressure valve is turned to seal.

4. Once beeper goes off, switch valve to vent and allow for natural pressure release.

5. After all, pressure has left, add in the remaining ingredients and click on Slow Cooker.

6. Stir all ingredients once over, close and lock lid. Cook on high pressure for 1 hour. Once beeper goes off, quick release pressure to stop cooking. Taste test and add salt and pepper if necessary.

7. Serve chili with a good dose of sour cream and garnish with freshly cut spring onions.

Buttery Mashed Potatoes

Total Preparation & Cook Time: 45 minutes

Servings – 4

Nutritional Info: Calories: 704, Fats: 71g, Carbs: 12g, Protein: 7.13g, Fiber: 0g, Sugar: 3.1g

Ingredients:

- 2 lb unpeeled red potatoes, cubed
- ¼ cup milk
- 4 tbsp butter
- ½ cup sour cream
- 1 tbsp minced garlic
- 1 tbsp chopped fresh parsley
- ½ tsp fresh basil
- 2 tsp salt
- 1 tsp pepper
- ¼ tsp dried oregano

Directions:

1. In your Instant Pot, add the chopped potatoes. Cover and cook the potatoes on Manual, high pressure for 40 minutes.

2. Once potatoes are cooked and tender, add all the remaining ingredients.

3. Use a masher to mash the potatoes and mix all ingredients till well combined.

4. Serve as a side to meat dishes.

Instant Pot Cheeseburger Sloppy Joes

Total Preparation & Cook Time: 45 minutes

Servings – 4

Nutritional Info: Calories: 1545, Fats: 116g, Carbs: 55g, Protein: 88.2g, Fiber: 6,4g, Sugar: 33g

Ingredients:

- 2 lb grass-fed beef
- 1 whole yellow onion diced
- 1 whole red bell pepper diced
- 14.5 oz canned tomatoes, drained and diced
- 1 ½ tsp barbecue seasoning
- 16 oz cheese
- 1 tsp dried oregano

Directions:

1. In your Instant Pot, click to Sauté and add the ground beef, diced onions, and diced bell peppers. Sauté until the meat is browned and onions are soft.
2. Drain pot to remove fat.
3. Mix well all remaining ingredients and stir well to combine.
4. Close and lock the lid, secure valve at and click on 'Meat' to cook on high pressure for 40 minutes.
5. When the pot starts beeping, cooking is over. Check to see if the veggies are tender and taste test.
6. Serve on hamburger buns.

Conclusion

Investing in an Instant Pot is one of the best things for your kitchen. This one single appliance makes cooking faster and so much more convenient. Foods that take a long time to cook now take only a fraction of the time. Busy parents to novice cooks can benefit from its fast cooking and young adults and those living in small apartments can definitely benefit from using this multi-cooking appliance to fit into cramped dorm rooms and small kitchens.

CPSIA information can be obtained
at www.ICGtesting.com
Printed in the USA
LVOW13s2156300317

529125LV00010B/645/P